ALSO BY STEPHEN MANSFIELD

Never Give In:
The Extraordinary Character of Winston Churchill

Faithful Volunteers:
The History of Religion in Tennessee

Then Darkness Fled:
The Liberating Wisdom of Booker T. Washington

More Than Dates and Dead People:
Recovering a Christian View of History

Forgotten Founding Father:
The Heroic Legacy of George Whitefield

The Faith of George W. Bush

Derek Prince: A Biography

THE FAITH

of the

AMERICAN SOLDIER

THE FAITH

of the

AMERICAN SOLDIER

STEPHEN MANSFIELD

Jeremy P. Tarcher / Penguin
a member of
Penguin Group (USA) Inc.

JEREMY P. TARCHER/PENGUIN
Published by the Penguin Group
Penguin Group (USA) Inc., 375 Hudson Street, New York, New York 10014, USA
Penguin Group (Canada), 90 Eglinton Avenue East, Suite 700, Toronto, Ontario
M4P 2Y3, Canada (a division of Pearson Penguin Canada Inc.)
Penguin Books Ltd, 80 Strand, London WC2R 0RL, England
Penguin Ireland, 25 St Stephen's Green, Dublin 2, Ireland
(a division of Penguin Books Ltd)
Penguin Group (Australia), 250 Camberwell Road, Camberwell,
Victoria 3124, Australia
(a division of Pearson Australia Group Pty Ltd)
Penguin Books India Pvt Ltd, 11 Community Centre, Panchsheel Park,
New Delhi–110 017, India
Penguin Group (NZ), Cnr Airborne and Rosedale Roads, Albany, Auckland 1310,
New Zealand (a division of Pearson New Zealand Ltd)
Penguin Books (South Africa) (Pty) Ltd, 24 Sturdee Avenue, Rosebank,
Johannesburg 2196, South Africa
Penguin Books Ltd, Registered Offices: 80 Strand, London WC2R 0RL, England

First trade paperback edition 2006

Copyright © 2005 by Stephen Mansfield
This book is being published jointly by Strang Communications and
Penguin Group (USA) Inc.

Cover photo © Scott Nelson/Getty Images
Cover design by Judith McKittrick
Author photo by Ben Pearson
Interior design by Terry Clifton

Most Tarcher/Penguin books are available at special quantity discounts for bulk
purchase for sales promotions, premiums, fund-raising, and educational needs.
Special books or book excerpts also can be created to fit specific needs.
For details, write Penguin Group (USA) Inc. Special Markets,
375 Hudson Street, New York, NY 10014.

An application to register this book for cataloging has been
submitted to the Library of Congress.
ISBN 1-58542-407-2
ISBN 1-58542-493-5 (paperback edition)

Printed in the United States of America
1 3 5 7 9 10 8 6 4 2

TO THE CHAPLAINS,

HEROES OF FAITH

WHO TEND THE WARRIOR SOUL

AUTHOR'S NOTE

The author has, in most cases, witnessed the episodes recounted. In some instances, interviews with eyewitnesses have been used. Some of the individuals in this book are composites of real persons, and some names have been changed to protect an individual's privacy or security. To avoid confusion to the reader, when the unit of a soldier is mentioned, the name used for him is his own. When the unit is not mentioned, that name has been changed at the soldier's request.

CONTENTS

THE VIGIL AT ARMS

There have always been rituals for welcoming men to the fellowship of arms. We read of them in Homer and *Beowulf*, in Cicero and the legends of King Arthur. Tacitus wrote of the Germans welcoming a young warrior to arms with the gift of a shield and a spear. Indeed, most every tribe and culture has had some ceremony that accompanied "the belting of the sword."

By the latter Middle Ages, though, the heritage of these early traditions had merged with the liturgies and offices of the Christian church to fashion a new kind of warrior called the knight. He was intended to be the perfect merging of holy passion and military might, of spiritual devotion and martial skill. His calling was the defense of Christendom, a task he could only expect to fulfill with a pure heart and a holy life. His war, then, was as much to master himself as it was with the enemies of the realm. In fact, he believed he would never succeed in serving his king until he first succeeded in serving his God.

A man was never born to knighthood. It was something he had to prove himself to be. Knights were fashioned in battle, honed by mentors, and disciplined by hardship. Knights were molded in the holy fires of spiritual seeking. And when the time was right and a man was chosen for the call, he prepared himself for the moment of his ascendance with a ritual all knights underwent: the Vigil.

The Vigil was the final ceremony of cleansing, of meditation, and of sacrifice. It was a purifying and resolving of the hungers of the heart. It was the liturgy by which a man who was simply a warrior became a knight in the service of God.

The Vigil began early on the day before a man was to be knighted. He was first bathed, usually in rose water and usually in a wooden tub. This signified his baptism, his reenactment of the burial of Jesus Christ in the tomb, and His resurrection to life again. The knight-to-be understood from this that he was no longer his own, that his life had been bought by the death of the Lord he now followed. His sins were cleansed. His heart made new. His affections fixed to a new allegiance.

As a sign of shed vanity, the man's hair was usually cut. In the Middle Ages, the sacrificing of one's hair was seen as a sign of devotion to God. This meant that a knight often wore his hair in the same crudely cut manner as a monk, reminding him that he had entered a calling more than an army, a holy order more than just a soldier's life.

xv

The knight candidate was then given new clothes. He first received a red garment with long sleeves and a hood that was placed over a white tunic. It was the symbol that this man was ready to shed his blood in the service of God and his king. Afterward a tight-fitting black coat was placed over the white and the red to signify that the knight should never fear death, which for the man of God is but reward.

Now properly cleansed and clothed, the man was taken to a chapel and left alone with his weapons and his armor. He had already begun a fast. It was a means of purifying both soul and body, humbling himself into his humanity, and reminding him always to champion the weak and the poor. Now, as a man clean in body and spirit, the knight-to-be presented himself to God.

With his companions and sponsors waiting prayerfully outside, the man spread his weapons on the altar and stood watch. For no less than ten hours, he prayed the prayers of devotion and ran his heart over each tool of his trade: his sword, his mace, his lance, his gauntlet, perhaps even his saddle and the standard of his king. And he waited. For God to receive him. For the words that would form his call. For the grace to conquer his passions. For the boldness befitting his charge.

He also envisioned the next day. His companions would come for him and take him to the appointed place. A priest would say a mass, and then the knight candidate would kneel. The priest would bless him, and then, while his companions held them aloft, the priest would bless his weapons.

There would be a sermon and charges from the older knights about the price of the call. Perhaps a pair of spurs would be put upon his feet, symbols of the nobility and rank he had attained. Certainly his mentors would attest to the other nobles that he was properly prepared, that his training was complete. And they would kiss him, in welcome to the fellowship of the sword.

The sword. Finally, it would be time. The sword crafted uniquely for him would be brought forth and laid before him. He had dreamed of the moment all his life. The priest would then take the sword, and the others might place their hands upon it as well. Then would come the sacred words:

> Bless this sword,
> so that it may be a defense
> for churches, widows, and orphans
> and for all servants of God
> against the fury of the heathen.

Then the king or the highest noble in attendance would administer the *collée*, the ceremonial blow to the head and neck with the sword. Later generations would remember this as a "dubbing," a tapping on the shoulders and head. In truth, it was more dramatic, more violent; it was a chopping motion meant to remind the knight that he was "under the sword," that he had already surrendered his life to a cause.

All this would come the next day. For now, though, the knight-to-be is in prayer, eager that he will never fail the holy trust he is about to receive. He is to be a knight: chosen, destined, anointed by his God. It is a sacred thing.

"Lord, make me worthy," he prays and then, in the concluding silence, *"Deus vult."* God wills it.

It is literally true—there are no atheists in foxholes—religion is precious under fire.

—LIEUTENANT GENERAL
A. A. VANDERGRIFT
FORMER COMMANDANT
UNITED STATES MARINE CORPS

INTRODUCTION

Lance Corporal James Gault sits trembling on the edge of his bunk somewhere in Iraq. His wet, reddened face is pressed firmly into his rugged hands. From time to time, he runs his palms over the short, blond hair that covers his scalp, as though driving his tears to the back of his skull.

Between sobs, Gault tells the chaplain his story. Just two days ago, his platoon drove their Humvees into a nearby village. It was just routine. They had been to the village many times. Gault had even come to recognize the faces of the children who gathered around their vehicles.

This time, though, the platoon came under attack. Insurgents had apparently entered the village and were now shooting from every direction. The Marines returned fire. Gault gripped his .50 caliber machine gun and searched the rooftops for the source of the rounds that were pinging against the sides of his Humvee. Then he saw it. There was a man firing a Kalashnikov from a roof just a few buildings away. Foolishly, the man fired down on the Marines from a standing position, which left him almost completely exposed.

Gault raised his gun and pressed the trigger. The massive weapon roared. Though he had been in the field for months, Gault was stunned by what happened next. The fierce barrage of the .50 caliber cut the man in half almost exactly at the waist. The Kalashnikov fell from his hands to the street three stories below. Then— as Gault watched in shock—the man's torso tilted forward, left his lower half, and fell to the street as well, not far from where Gault crouched in his vehicle. The man's legs and mid-section still stood upright on the roof, just as they had when the man was alive.

For two days, the scene has refused to leave James Gault's mind. He replays it again and again—and it forces him against the greater realities of his life. Gault is no coward. Nor is he the kind of easily shaken, sensitive soul who cannot endure the horrors of war. He has killed, and he will kill again. In fact, he believes "the bad guys *have* to die." To kill in a righteous cause is what Gault has come to Iraq to do, and he does not shrink from the charge.

Yet, Gault is also a Christian, a man who believes that Jesus is God, that He rose from the dead, and that the Bible is the truth of God for all men. He can remember that his lifelong dream of becoming a Marine somehow grew naturally from his southern Christian upbringing—from life in his Baptist church, from the prayers his high school football coach led, from the mealtime preaching of his farmer father, from the love of country that filled every heart and home in the town where he was born. James Gault is a Christian and a warrior. This is his destiny.

He remembers clearly the Sunday his family went to church just hours before he was to catch his plane for Iraq. His mother had begged him to wear his dress uniform, and though he was embarrassed at the thought, he finally agreed. Once the service began, the pastor called Gault and his parents forward and told the congregation that they were going to pray, reminding them to continue to intercede "for our young hero while he is overseas." Then the pastor, along with the Gault family and leaders of the church, laid their hands on James's shoulders and prayed for safety, for courage, and that "Lord, You would make his hands skillful to battle Your enemies."

 Now, sitting on the edge of his bunk, Gault can remember the sense of honor and pride he felt that day—and he wants it back. Ripping a man in half with his weapon has shaken him to his core, his foundation, the radiating truths of his life. He knows he is a follower of Jesus, and he knows that he is called to be a Marine, but the violence he unleashed leaves him needing assurance that he has killed in a righteous cause, that his country is doing the will of God in Iraq.

Tormented, Gault talks to his chaplain, a naval officer he knows to be a good man. "Tell me that our enemies are the enemies of God," Gault pleads. "Explain to me how this is a war between good and evil."

The chaplain is startled by the request. "I cannot tell you that the other side is evil," the chaplain says calmly. "Our government is officially nonreligious, and so are our armed forces. We do not fight holy wars. We do not view our enemies in religious terms. I can tell you that you fight for a great nation, though, and that God is with you if you turn your heart to Him."

Gault is not comforted. He is seeking something more. He needs a moral vision, a confidence that he killed in the service of good, no matter the horror and no matter the price. He has not found it, and now he is undone.

"I need to know," he says hoarsely, almost in prayer, "that I am a servant of Jesus. I need to be sure that I am a soldier of Christ."

In the same platoon is Lance Corporal Darrin McKay. Thickly muscled and plastered with tattoos, McKay is a smaller, meaner-looking version of Arnold Schwarzenegger. If the artwork needled into his skin is any guide, he has spent his life among the "bad and the bold" answering his thirst for women and danger. His credo adorns his left arm: "Though I walk through the valley of the shadow of death, I shall fear no evil, for I am the baddest warrior in the valley."

McKay tells everyone who will listen that he is in Iraq because "when the going gets tough, the tough go Marine." He joined up after high school in Los Angeles because he wanted to experience *"Fear Factor* on stun," a reference to the popular television show in which contestants confront their fears to win prizes. Nicknamed "Sparky" by the other men of the platoon because he is short and squat like a spark plug, McKay sees life as a series of challenges to his personal toughness. He doesn't fight for nation or ideals. He suspects that the politicians who sent him to Iraq are no less corrupt than the dealers on the streets of L.A. He doesn't care. He is here to prove himself and to return home as "bad as any mother's son who ever walked the earth."

McKay's day is testament to testosterone. He lifts weights while vowing to tear the head from the next "raghead" he sees with his bare hands. He cleans his rifle while speaking to it like a lover. This irritates his fellow Marines, but everyone knows you don't cross McKay. On patrol, he is a cussing, raging machine, stoked for combat by the coffee crystals he packs in his cheeks like chewing tobacco, by the ephedrine he took back at camp, and by the visceral fierceness he has honed in the conflicts of his life.

McKay's only real friend is a black kid the men call "Dogman." He is the "cool" everyone wants to be, a grooving, laughing tough from the streets of Detroit who is as good a Marine as any man in the platoon. And for some reason that no one can explain, McKay loves him. Perhaps their friendship started when Dogman showed he wasn't afraid of McKay, or perhaps it happened when McKay was in a bad mood in the bar-

6

racks one evening but Dogman pulled him up for a buck dance to an OutKast tune anyway. McKay couldn't keep his "mad on," and everyone shouted rowdy cheers as the two did their thing. Something started that night, and everyone knows McKay and Dogman are "tight," that McKay would kill a man who messed with that skinny, smiling black kid.

Then it happened. One night McKay and Dogman were keeping an eye on the entrance to a house with five other Marines while a second squad entered from the rear. The night was quiet. Men joked and cussed, never taking their eyes from the gated entrance to the house across the street. Dogman was just a few feet behind McKay and was just telling him how stupid white boys from L.A. are when the mortar round hit. It landed behind Dogman and nearly vaporized him, spraying the now unrecognizable matter of his body all over McKay. The surviving Marines dragged each other behind a wall, and it was then that McKay realized he was sticky with his friend's lifeblood, and that the white matter embedded in the crease on his left arm was the eye of the friend he loved so well.

It is a week later now. McKay is slumped over coffee at the camp watering hole, the fire and the anger gone from his chiseled face. He grieves for his friend, but there is something more. Death, which has always seemed at bay from his strong, arrogant life, is now as close as his breath. He will end; someday, somehow, he will end. Just as Dogman left this life, so will McKay. And he knows it now. This body he has worked so hard to craft, this persona he has come to love so much, it will all end and probably in a bloody crush here in Iraq.

Death is asking Darrin McKay who he is and what he believes. But he does not know. "Dogman was the best of us," McKay says quietly, refusing a tear, "and he went in an instant. I probably will, too. But I wish I knew something about what's on the other side. I wish I believed something or I had done something that makes it all worthwhile. I hate the thought of dying, but I hate the thought of dying empty most of all."

As these tales from the Iraqi frontlines portray, wars press questions of faith into the lives of those who fight them. It has been so throughout history. From the moment nations commit themselves to armed conflict until the last shot is fired, wars move men to strengthen their grasp on the invisible realities that define their lives—and in a way that is unmatched by any other human endeavor. This is a story that is seldom told in our secular age, but it is among the most inspiring and instructive sagas the history of men at arms has to offer.

When soldiers step upon the battlefield, they immediately confront the kind of horror and hardship that has moved men through the centuries to reach for the spiritual. There is the loneliness and the fear, the boredom and the rage. Death surrounds them. Comrades die horribly. The specter of their own demise haunts every step. There is the dread of killing another human being, known to be among the greatest fears of fighting men. Daily, the pageant of human folly is played out before them, searing into memory the lessons of man's weakness and transience in this world. Each of these drive men to the invisible; each forces the soldier to decide what he truly believes, making the battlefield as much a test of faith as it is a test of arms.

This has been as true of the war in Iraq as it has been of other wars in history. Not long after the start of Operation Iraqi Freedom on March 20, 2003, amid the reports of victory and death, tales of faith arose from the battlefields. Newspapers reported Bible studies, prayer meetings, and standing-room-only worship services in the American camps. Magazines ran photos of Marines being baptized in the Euphrates River and fully armed soldiers kneeling in prayer before going on patrol. There were accounts of a worship service on the eve of the battle for Fallujah with Christian rock music blaring and uniformed worshipers raising their hands in praise of their God. Some chaplains who had served in earlier conflicts reported that they had never before seen such spiritual hunger among troops at war. Clearly, the crucible of war was turning the American soldier to seek out his God.

Yet, as comforted as Americans at home must have been by these reports, they were soon faced with other, more disturbing images. In Michael Moore's controversial film *Fahrenheit 9/11*, a critical examination of the Bush administration, young soldiers were shown discussing what hard rock song they preferred to hear on the sound system of their tank when invading a village. The unspoken message seemed clear: there is a new, more brazen, less principled generation at war. Some experts began discussing the new pagan ethos of the American military. Pictures of U.S. soldiers mistreating Iraqis at Abu Ghraib prison seemed to prove the point.

Equally disturbing was the furor over statements by Lieutenant General William Boykin, the deputy undersecretary of defense for intelligence. In a series of talks in churches and later explanations to the press, Boykin, a highly decorated three-star general and an evangelical Christian, referred to U.S. forces as a "Christian army." He also suggested that George W. Bush had been placed in office by God, that America is hated abroad because of her Christianity, and that the war against terrorism is paralleled by a spiritual war between good and evil. Though many Americans thought that these were the very beliefs the nation should want her warriors to hold, the general's words stirred such controversy that some elected leaders called for his resignation. President Bush even found it necessary to assure Muslim clerics that Boykin's views weren't the views of the nation.

Suddenly, America seemed to be wrestling with the role religion has to play in her military culture. For some, this came as no surprise. At the time, the country was wrestling with questions of faith in nearly every area of her national life, and for a simple reason: America is a nation religiously in tension with herself. While a vast majority of her citizens believe in God, attend worship regularly, and see their country in religious terms, the institutions of American government are required— under force of recent Supreme Court decisions—to lean religiously neutral if not secular. This produces some strange inconsistencies, largely due to the cultural imprint of the nation's Christian heritage. The Ten Commandments may not be posted in public schools, but the United States Congress employs a Christian chaplain. The Pledge of Allegiance may some day not include the words "one nation under God," but "In God

We Trust" is printed on the national currency. Families may not pray at high school football games, but presidents pray in the Oval Office. It is a confusing brew.

Not surprisingly, these religious tensions in American culture are keenly felt by many in the military. Warrior culture demands clarity. It tends to intensify and refine the values of a society, forcing them into stark simplicity. Soldiers must know, in clear terms, not only why they fight but also if their cause is just, moral, righteous, even holy. This is all the more necessary in the modern war on terror, where the enemy is a religious network citing religious reasons for aggression. Yet while the modern soldier may personally be as religious as he wants to be, his country forbids him from publicly defining his fight in religious terms or understanding himself as an agent of faith. For many, this is a break both from the flow of faith in American history and from the faith that has shaped the Western military tradition for centuries.

No one feels these tensions as keenly as military chaplains. Though it is their job to tend the spiritual needs of warriors and their families, they nevertheless serve as an arm of the secular state. They may preach the sermons, counsel the hurting, and care for the wounded and dying, but they may not frame their nation's wars in spiritual terms or suggest that the religions of their enemies are inferior to their own. For many chaplains, this is a frustrating restriction, particularly when the soldiers they serve face the rage of Muslim jihadists who oppose America for religious reasons.

This is also a frustration for those chaplains who understand the nature of a warrior code and the legacy of faith that has fashioned that code in Western history. Though warrior codes have arisen in most every culture strong enough to sustain one, the Western code is drawn from the Christian heritage of chivalry and the knightly traditions that have left their mark even to this day. The salute, the epaulet, and even military chaplains themselves are vestiges of this heritage. Yet, if these are all that remain of this grand tradition, what has been lost, and at what cost?

Indeed, this larger question suggests still others: In a modern, secular military, who fashions the warrior's code, and what should that code be? What is it that lives in a soldier as he or she enters battle that defines purpose, fashions the moral self, and determines the ethics of combat? Perhaps more, where does it come from? Are the moral pronouncements of presidents and preachers enough? Are "Rules of Engagement" all that an officially secular society can offer its defenders? Is this sufficient in an age of limited wars, police actions, and terrorists holding civilian populations hostage?

Are we risking more My Lai massacres and more Abu Ghraib scandals for the lack of a faith-based code of military conduct? Has a time-tested warrior code been driven from American military culture in the pursuit of a religiously neutral society?

What follows in these pages is an attempt to answer these questions by way of exploring and celebrating the religious nature of America's military heritage. This is not to be confused, though, with a celebration of war. Only the immoral or the deformed of soul can exalt war itself, with all of the grinding horrors that it brings.

Instead, this book is the product of a search for the meaning of the American warrior code and the faith that gave it birth. It is a search that has taken the author and his research team from the battlefields of Iraq to "the plain" of West Point, from the home of the 101st Airborne at Fort Campbell, Kentucky, to the headquarters of USCENTCOM at MacDill Air Force Base in Tampa, Florida. It has progressed through dozens of interviews with men and women who have heroically served in their country's wars, and it has continued in the great body of the world's military literature.

It is a search, though, that is well worth the journey. A nation's warrior code is an extension of its soul, the embodiment of its highest ideals. There can be few more noble tasks than to understand that code and to honor it as the distilled greatness of a people. Such is the guiding dream of this book.

The war was a mirror; it reflected

man's every virtue and every vice, and

if you looked closely, like an artist at

his drawings, it showed up both with

unusual clarity.

—GEORGE GROSZ (1893–1959)
GERMAN ARTIST

C HAPTER 1

THE NEW GENERATION AT WAR

I t was March 27, 2003, one week after the

bombardment of Baghdad had begun, the

start of Operation Iraqi Freedom. For an elite

force of Army Rangers and the 173rd Airborne

Brigade, though, the war was just beginning.

THE FAITH OF THE AMERICAN SOLDIER

Their assignment was to parachute by night to a point just outside of Mosul and prepare to support the invasion from deep within Iraq. It was a dangerous mission, one that required a treacherous "night drop." This meant jumping out of the back of a C-130 from high altitude and falling in complete darkness to as near the earth as possible before opening their chutes. Once on the ground, they would await reinforcements and then move to secure the strategic oil fields in Kirkuk. They had done it and done it well. With a skill born of tireless training and long experience, they had then gone about the business of preparing to liberate Iraq.

In the few moments of reflection they had, some of them looked down on Mosul from a nearby hill and knew its secret. This was no common Iraqi town. The ancient name for Mosul was Nineveh, and it had been the chief city of the Assyrians. Kings with names like Sargon, Sennacherib, and Ashurbanipal ruled from this place. In fact, one of the most beloved stories from the Bible involved this very city, the story of Jonah. Every child in Sunday school knew that Jonah had refused to preach in Nineveh because he hated the Assyrians and didn't want them to repent and escape the judgment of God. So he tried to run away. He boarded a ship and sailed westward across the Mediterranean, but he ended up inside a huge fish that spewed him out on the great sea's eastern shore. Jonah then changed his mind and preached God's message to Nineveh.

But there is more to the story. The Book of Jonah tells us that the prophet was so infuriated at the idea that his hated enemy might receive God's mercy that he sat on the side of a hill overlooking Nineveh and forced himself in rage to watch. Jonah was, as he told his God, "angry enough to die." What he feared came to pass. The Ninevites repented; God in His mercy spared them the judgment they deserved; and Jonah—sitting upon a hillside some distance from the city—bitterly saw it all.

Centuries later, on that same hillside, American soldiers prepared to free the people of Iraq. And, as they went about their duties, they too were visited by messengers of God, for their chaplains had accompanied them on their perilous mission. Moving quietly from unit to unit, these chaplains—unarmed but for the Bibles in their hands—gave mini-sermons to the men, challenged them to trust in God, and prayed with those who wanted something more.

Before the invasion of Iraq began, several hundred of the men positioned on the hills outside of Mosul had devoted their hearts and their cause to Jesus Christ. It was an astonishing embrace of faith, and even the chaplains themselves were amazed. Yet this was not the last time that American soldiers in Iraq would turn to the faith of their fathers, to the religion that was born, in part, in the very land their Humvees now carried them across. In fact, the American troops in Iraq would take hold of religion as much as any army had in the nation's history. The conversions on a hill outside of Mosul were just the beginning.

The American engagements in Afghanistan and Iraq are proving to be among the most unique military actions in the nation's history. This is, in part, because a volunteer U.S. military has never before been engaged in armed conflict overseas for this length of time. Nor has the nation ever faced the challenge of rebuilding a devastated country on the heels of such a decisive military victory and in an Islamic culture. Yet the wars in Afghanistan and Iraq are also unique because there is a new generation of Americans fighting them, a generation that is transforming the face of America at war.

They are the youngest children of the generation that fought in Vietnam, the grandchildren and great-grandchildren of those who fought in World War II. Most of them were born in the early 1980s, which means that the only wars they can remember outside of movies and books are the conflict in Kosovo and America's brief but tragic involvement in Somalia made popular by the film *Black Hawk Down*. Called everything from Generation X to Millennials to Echo Boomers, they are as difficult to define as they are to name.

They were not expected to do well. The conventional wisdom pegged them as the spoiled offspring of guilt-ridden baby-boomer parents who plied them with toys but never told them who they really were. They lived, we were told, in a materialistic, amoral, "online" world that hardened their souls and sickened their minds. Studies repeatedly warned that these Millennials—the most popular name for this generation who came of age around the dawn of the new century—held no absolutes, built monuments to the carnal and impure, and were sure to be the new barbarians pressing at the gates of Western civilization. They gave us Columbine, after all, and a dozen other symbols of decadence and decline.

When they first appeared on their nation's battlefield, observers insisted on viewing them against this darker, more nihilistic image before they had a chance to prove otherwise. *Rolling Stone* reporter Evan Wright, who accompanied some of the first Marines into Iraq and recorded his observations in an essential book called *Generation Kill*, described the new generation at war as "kids raised on hip-hop, Marilyn Manson and Jerry Springer" for whom "slain rapper Tupac is an

American patriot whose writings are better known than the speeches of Abraham Lincoln."[1] In Wright's view, cynicism rules these new Millennials at war:

> ...if the dominant mythology [is] that war turns on a generation's loss of innocence—young men reared on *Davy Crockett* waking up to their government's deceits while fighting in Southeast Asian jungles; the nation falling from the grace of Camelot to the shame of Watergate—these young men entered Iraq predisposed toward the idea that the Big Lie is as central to American governance as taxation. Even though their Commander in Chief tells them they are fighting today in Iraq to protect American freedom, few would be shaken to discover that they might actually be leading a grab for oil. In a way, they almost expect to be lied to.[2]

22

What Wright described in print, Michael Moore painted on the big screen. In his film *Fahrenheit 9/11*, Moore included a particularly disturbing interview with young soldiers in Iraq, still wide-eyed at the brilliant horrors of war. After discussing how "innocent civilians" are often killed and why American troops "pretty much at first shot anything that moved," the eager warriors then described how rock music prepares them for action.

> *American Soldier #1*: "It's the ultimate rush cuz you know you're going into the fight to begin with, and then you got a good song playing in the background and, uh, that gets you real fired up. Ready to do the job."

> *American Soldier #2*: "You can hook your CD player up to the tank's internal communications..."

> *American Soldier #3*: "To the Charlie Box..."

> *American Soldier #2*: "...so that way when you put your helmet on you can hear it through the helmet."

> *American Soldier #4*: "This is the one we listen to the most. This is the one we travel, we kill the enemy (pointing to Drowning Pool CD). Drowning Pool, 'Let the Bodies Hit the Floor,' is just fitting for the job that we're doing."

> *American Soldier #5*: "We picked 'The
> Roof Is On Fire' because, uh, basically it
> symbolized Baghdad bein' on fire and, uh,
> and at the time we wanted it to burn to
> get Saddam and his regime out. The roof
> is on fire…we don't need no water…let
> [it]…burn."

The verdict seemed clear. The people fighting America's battles were drugged-up mall rats with machine guns, the Columbine killers now sent abroad to murder the innocents of other lands and all to the sound of a carefully chosen heavy metal song. No one seemed to expect the new generation at war to have any connection to a moral vision for their conflict. It was doubtful they would even be capable of understanding it. This was, after all, the generation that one survey portrayed as thinking that Central America was somewhere near Kansas. As one sergeant complained, "All the press seemed to hope for us was that we would somehow kill more of the enemy than we would our own soldiers."

It was not long, though, before the Millennials began to reveal their more noble self. Something happened—perhaps the horrors of September 11, 2001, or a generation rising to its country's need or maybe a chance to fight for something more than a parking space at the mall—that changed them and defied both their his-

24

tory and their critics. As military historian Victor Davis Hanson wrote, "The general critique of the 1990s was that we had raised a generation with peroxide hair and tongue rings, general illiterates who lounged at malls, occasionally muttering 'like' and 'you know' in Sean Penn or Valley Girl cadences. But somehow the military has married the familiarity and dynamism of crass popular culture to nineteenth-century notions of heroism, self-sacrifice, patriotism, and audacity."[3] This comment and others like it were the early indications that the Millennials at war were about to shine.

It turned out that the conventional wisdom was wrong. It had said, for example, that the Millennials were mocking pessimists who found most politicians more akin to game show hosts than statesmen and who intended to "rage against the machine." The truth is that the new generation trusted their government more than their boomer parents did at the same age. A 1975 Harris Poll reported that only 20 percent of people ages eighteen to twenty-nine expressed any confidence in those who ran the military.[4] By 2002, though, a poll conducted by the Harvard Institute of Politics found that 70 percent of college undergraduates trusted the military to "do the right thing either most or all of the time."[5]

The caricature of the typical Millennial also suggested an uninformed slacker who knew little of the world and less of his own country's meaning. This too proved false. The average soldier at war in 2002 was 21.1 years old. This meant he was a bit older than many realized and had some college experience. He was also better informed about his world than any generation that has been called upon to fight its nation's wars. Soldiers in Iraq and Afghanistan are seldom far from Fox News or CNN broadcasts, and most have access to the Internet, where both websites and e-mails from home keep them abreast of world events.

The image of the Millennials as fighters without moral vision proved false as well. This expectation may have been a holdover from previous generations, though. For some time, the academic consensus was that soldiers do not fight for ideology but for each other. The military-speak for this is "unit cohesion," which commanders expected would be a high motivation for Millennials, the generation that lauds community almost above morals and has made the "hang out and hook up," Starbucks-type establishment a raging success.

History seemed to support this view. One study of Confederate soldiers during the Civil War concluded, "It is doubtful whether many of them either understood or cared about the Constitutional issues at stake."[6] A similar examination of Union soldiers revealed, "One searches most letters and diaries in vain for soldiers'

comment on why they were in the war or for what they were fighting."[7] Even among "the greatest generation," few were found in the 1940s who thought philosophically about their conflict. The leading study of their thinking concluded that, "Officers and enlisted men alike attached little importance to idealistic motives—patriotism and concern about war aims."[8]

The Millennials broke from this history. Not only had many of them enlisted during a high tide of post–September 11 patriotism, but also the task of defeating a dictator and rebuilding a country was easy to understand in ideological terms. A study by the Strategic Studies Institute of the U.S. Army War College, entitled *Why They Fight: Combat Motivation in the Iraq War*, concluded, "In the present study, many soldiers *did* respond that they were motivated by idealistic notions. Liberating the people and bringing freedom to Iraq were common themes in describing their combat motivation." In the words of one soldier, "Liberating those people. Liberating Iraq. Seeing them free. They were repressed for, I don't know how many years, thirty something years. Just knowing that they are free now. Knowing that is awesome to me."[9]

27

Even journalists, schooled on the conventional image of the new soldier, were amazed. One embedded journalist reported, "Soldiers I encountered were trained, ethical, thoughtful, and intelligent. It was not unusual to talk to a private or private first class and be absolutely astounded at how well he could talk about why they were there."[10] Another journalist, moved by his experience with young soldiers at the front, insisted, "The press back home doesn't have it right. We are doing these people a disservice. I haven't found *Animal House* and *Debbie Does Dallas* over here. What I found was *Braveheart* and *Saving Private Ryan*."

The Millennials, then, have defied both their programming and their nation's expectations. A dormant greatness has begun to arise in them, and they may well, before the present war is over, prove that they have, indeed, stood upon the shoulders of the greatest generation.

They are, however, doing war in their own uniquely millennial fashion. Nothing reveals this like the culture of the American military camps that now dot the landscape in Afghanistan and Iraq.

The ghost of a soldier from the Second World War would stroll the American camps in Iraq amazed. Certainly his mind would strain to understand the technology that has transformed the nature of modern warfare. From the night-vision equipment that adorns the front of a Marine's helmet to laser-guided missile systems, from the overwhelming air power his nation now has to the almost miraculous lightness of a soldier's body armor, the visitor from World War II would quickly realize that war today is far from what he knew.

Yet he would likely be most astonished by the new brand of warrior and the culture that surrounds him. The Millennials are as serious as any soldiers who have taken the field in an American cause, but they retain a casual approach to life that makes them seem, at times—normal. The Army allows soldiers away from the front to wear regulation warm-up suits in camp. Combine this with the modern replacement of the duffel bag—the Army-issue black backpack—and a group of soldiers moving through Camp Victory just outside of Baghdad, for example, might look like any band of students on any American college campus leaving the gym for the school library. The impression lasts, though, only until a rocket attack occurs. Then the impressive skills of these warriors surface.

In many ways, the soldiers in the field are indeed just like their college counterparts at home. At the larger camps—with names like Liberty, Anaconda, and Victory—soldiers eat in facilities that put some college cafeterias to shame. At Camp Victory, for example, the DFAC—military shorthand for "dining facility"—is a grand affair the size of many college gymnasiums where a soldier may eat as much as he wishes of twelve or fifteen different courses and then return to his tent or trailer with soft drinks and protein bars in hand. Sitting in chatty groups and clothed in their warm-up suits, these soldiers often seem no different from a similar band at any American school until, that is, a look at the floor reveals their M4 rifle, the carbine version of the M16, lying at their feet.

Just like at home, a television is rarely far away. While soldiers dine at Camp Victory, large-screen airings of Skynews, MSNBC, CNN, and Fox are always in view. For the first time in American history, soldiers at war see the same daily news reports their parents do at home. Indeed, so politically charged is the atmosphere around them that some who seldom had a political thought while in the states find themselves becoming political junkies in the field. If an argument breaks out at a DFAC table, it is likely to be about whether Sean Hannity or Al Franken is closer to the truth. Sports is the other passion. Rarely is a meal to be had at some of the larger camps when a loud groan or cheer is not heard over some happening in the world of sports back home.

This love of sports feeds a passion for fitness that makes the health craze in the states pale by comparison. The camps are strewn with magazines like *Men's Fitness* and *Shape*, and the shelves at the Post Exchange are heavy with protein powders, weight-lifting gloves, and the newest replacement for ephedrine. Fitness equipment is modern and profuse. This is clearly by design. American soldiers in Afghanistan and Iraq are not allowed to drink alcohol in deference to the Muslim culture of the countries they are liberating. For the same reason, they may not look at pornography or, due to military law, have sex with fellow servicemen and women. This makes the gym or a pick-up game of basketball or football an invaluable release. "It helps," said one captain, "but I do sometimes wish we were liberating a less restrictive culture—like the French, maybe."

The hours not filled with duty and fitness are usually eased by some form of technology. Digital cameras, iPods, mini-DVD players, CD players, computers, Internet cameras, and even cell phones are everywhere. A group of medics with no pressing business watch Tom Cruise on the mini-DVD player atop an unused gurney. A military policeman in Afghanistan downloads a file his family attached to an e-mail and watches it on his notebook computer. A Ranger listens on his iPod to a recording of his mother recounting family news. He downloaded her voice from the family website and replays it for comfort while he is in the field. When the news is filled with reports of fighting in their region, soldiers often rush to the Internet cameras atop the computers the Army provides to assure their families they are fine.

The new technologies are creating problems undreamed of in other wars. A soldier's blog—his online journal or weblog—might accidentally contain classified information. What is his superior to do? The digital camera a chopper pilot carries in the cargo pocket of his fatigues might include pictures that would help his captors locate targets inside one of the camps. How does a commander assure security?

Then there is the tragic side of rapid communication back home. Not too many months into the Iraq war, a young Marine was killed, and those who fought at his side were naturally devastated. One of these carried a WorldPhone, a cell phone that can receive signal anywhere in the world. Needing comfort, the young Marine called his wife and told her about his friend's death just minutes before. The Marine's wife then foolishly called the wife of the dead soldier, who, of course, had not yet been contacted by the Marine Corps and was devastated both by the news and by the way she was informed. Given that it sometimes took weeks and even months to inform a family of a death in earlier wars, this is a new and disorienting crisis of speed.

Yet, of all the ways Millennials are changing America at war, their unique approach to religion must rank among the most important. This is truly unexpected. Some experts are surprised to find that this new generation has any religion at all. They are, after all, the children of the baby boomers who first rejected traditional faith—it was their generation that wondered if God was dead in the mid-sixties—and then began to surf every possible religious wave their times had to offer.

The first hint on the battlefield that a new brand of warrior was seeking a vital faith in the field was during the Gulf War. The elder brothers and sisters of those fighting in Iraq and Afghanistan today began to seek God and a spiritual understanding of their task in ways and in numbers that were astonishing less than two decades after the aching irreligion of the Vietnam era.

During Operation Desert Shield, for example, some 18,474 soldiers from the XVIII Airborne Corps attended religious services. The U.S. Army Central Command (ARCENT) sponsored 7,946 religious meetings with an attendance of 341,344 soldiers. This evidence of a new religious fervor moved Major General Barry McCaffrey to remark that "we had the most religious Army since the Army of Northern Virginia during the Civil War."[11]

By the time the Millennials began to serve their country a decade later, they had already begun to merge the spiritual passion of their elder brothers and sisters with a creatively nontraditional approach to faith. Some have called this *postmodern faith*, and some have called it *unchurched faith*. However it is named, it is becoming a defining mark of Millennials at war.

The surprising phenomenon of the Millennials' approach to religion, of the American twenty-somethings' spiritual search, is its level of intensity and passion. Some have interpreted this in terms of the times. This generation has come of age in a post–September 11 world in which religious faith has become more central to American culture than it was for their parents. Following September 11, 2001, religious slogans were emblazoned on milk cartons, and members of Congress who would have fought to the death for the separation of church and state nevertheless stood on the steps of the nation's capital and sang "God Bless America."

There is also the encouragement of popular culture to consider. From presidents who speak openly of being born again to rappers who thank Jesus Christ at award shows, faith has received new emphasis in nearly every stream of society. Medical doctors attend seminars on faith and healing, leading magazines offer front-page articles on the divinity of Jesus or the latest discoveries of biblical archaeologists, and corporate America revisits the role of faith in productivity. Mel Gibson's film *The Passion of the Christ* has become the most-watched presentation of Christian truth in history, and books that normally would never make it out of the Christian publishing ghetto—*The Prayer of Jabez, The Purpose-Driven Life,* and Tim LaHaye's Left Behind series, for example—sell millions in the mainstream markets. Clearly the Millennials arrived at adulthood during an explosion of interest in religion and faith, and this has only launched them further in their own search for truth.

There are some, though, who see the religious passion of the Millennials as the heart cry of a troubled generation. The statistics tell the tale. Some one-fourth to one-third of all Millennials live in single-parent families. More than half of these single parents have unmarried partners living with them.[12] Not surprisingly, nearly half of this generation has been sexually active during their teen years.[13] It is not hard to imagine that the spiritual hunger of Millennials is, in part, their response to the unstable lives their boomer parents bequeathed to them.

Whatever the source, the fact is that the Millennials are a generation of spiritual seekers—but only of a nontraditional variety. In keeping with their postmodern ways, they have rejected the structures, doctrines, and

35

standards of traditional faith in pursuit of spiritual experience, loving community, and stories that have power to define their lives. Some Christian analysts have called this "love the gospel, hate the church." Millennials seem to love the person of Jesus but run from the churches that preach in His name. They want a community defined by faith, but they find the traditional church too performance-oriented, too much a pastor's personality cult, and too removed from the realities of their daily lives to be of any use to them. As one analyst has said, "If the church in America doesn't get more relevant to the Millennials, the future of millennial faith is going to be five people gathered around a table at Starbucks drinking lattes and poring over a copy of *Purpose-Driven Something or Other*."

Yet these trends are more a commentary on the Millennials' collision with boomer spirituality than it is on the state of faith in the younger generation. More than eight out of ten Millennials said that their religious faith is very important in their life, and a majority of Millennials claim to have committed their lives to Jesus Christ.[14] Three quarters of them pray at least once a week, and more than half read their Bibles or some form of religious literature regularly. Perhaps more important, Millennials tend to view life more in spiritual, even mystical, terms than earlier generations. This is in part due to the power of film and television and in part due to the bankruptcy of the purely rationalistic worldview in their generation. But it means that while Millennials may not devote themselves to the traditions of faith, they are eager to understand life in terms of the spiritual realities of faith.

Sometimes this leads to a kind of utilitarian spirituality, what some have called a "faith buffet" or a "whatever works" kind of religion. When one Millennial was asked what he believed, he said, "One part Buddha, three parts Jesus, two parts fortune cookie, and three parts Oprah." The surprise of this statement is that the one who made it was so self-aware. Most Millennials acquire their religions much as they catch colds: through casual contact with strangers. The result is a pastiche of faith that is not only without system but also often without cohesion.

This, then, is the state of the Millennials' faith. Many are eager for spirituality but suspicious of institutions, hungry for truth but bored by systematics, inspired by stories but repelled by standards, desperate for religious experience but put off by religious style, hoping for spiritual family but disgusted by empty conformity, longing for God but wondering if He is there.

And now they are at war, and war, as it has through centuries, is pressing them to define themselves religiously more clearly than they ever have before. In this they are not unlike the young Winston Churchill. After escaping from a prisoner of war camp during the Boer War in South Africa, Churchill quickly discovered that the fashionable atheism he had adopted before the war now failed him. Alone and in constant danger as he escaped through Boer territory, he turned to the faith of his youth and found himself singing the songs and saying the prayers his Christian nanny had taught him years before.

It was a permanent turning point in his life. In a matter of hours he renewed his grip on the faith of his fathers and never let go. He later told the story of this awakening in his autobiography, *My Early Life*.

> I found no comfort in any of the philosophical ideas which some men parade in their hours of ease and strength and safety. They seemed only fair-weather friends. I realized with awful force that no exercise of my own feeble wit and strength could save me from my enemies, and that without the assistance of that High Power which interferes in the eternal sequence of causes and effects more often than we are always prone to

admit, I could never succeed. I prayed long and earnestly for help and guidance. My prayer, as it seems to me, was swiftly and wonderfully answered.[15]

Many of the Millennials in Afghanistan and Iraq today are experiencing much the same turning to a more defined faith. War forces a definition of belief. It strips away the superficial and even the cultural and leaves only what is relevant in the face of death, horror, and fear. War filters, refines, and distills. It is unforgiving of superficiality, easy answers, and thin religiosity. It presses against faith with a driving practicality, with a demand for real-world meaning. Religion on the battlefield has to "work," has to prove its worth in results.

It is this very filtering that makes the spirituality of Millennials perfectly suited for adaptation to the battlefield. They are already utilitarian in their religion. They want what works no matter where it comes from or how it is applied. They don't mind borrowing meaningful practices from any faith. The presence of Millennials on the battlefield, then, means the rise of a religious free market, a crashing world of faith experimentation that not only says much about Millennial culture but may also reveal much about the future condition of religion in the world.

The soldier, above all other men, is required to practice the greatest act of religious training—sacrifice. In battle and in the face of danger and death, he discloses those divine attributes which his Maker gave when He created man in His own image. No physical courage and no brute instinct can take the place of the divine help which alone can sustain him.

—General Douglas MacArthur
(1880–1964)
in his famous "Duty, Honor, Country"
speech at West Point, 1962

CHAPTER 2

SHIELDS OF STRENGTH

I t was April 3, 2003, and the United

States had been in Iraq for almost two

weeks. Captain Russell Rippetoe, along

with Staff Sergeant Nino Livaudais, age

twenty-three, and Specialist Ryan P. Long,

age twenty-one, were inspecting cars with

other soldiers of their company at a checkpoint some two hours outside of Baghdad. It was important work, and they knew it. Near the checkpoint they guarded was a dam. If the insurgents were allowed to get close to that dam and blow it up, the villages nearby would be flooded. People would die, and the cause of liberty, which Captain Rippetoe and his team saw as their mission, would suffer a serious blow. They went about their duties as though peace in the world depended upon it.

But then Russell Rippetoe had always lived life like a man on a mission. He was, after all, a member of the 75th Ranger Regiment, the unit whose heroism lives in modern memory through the film *Black Hawk Down*. Rippetoe wanted to live up to that reputation. It had bothered him, for example, that he hadn't had a chance to make a parachute jump into the Baghdad airport when his unit arrived in Iraq. The planned jump was abandoned, and Rippetoe and his team had made a normal runway landing. "I wanted to jump to see if I would hold up to the stress," he wrote in his journal, "and do my job to the standard of all the Rangers."

Rippetoe was always achieving, always striving to be the man of his inner vision. A soccer star, the homecoming king at his Colorado high school, and an Eagle Scout, he had hoped to fly planes for the Air Force. His dyslexia killed that dream, though, and he decided

42

instead to attend the University of Colorado, where he majored in management. After a few years he began eyeing the Army, and when he joined after graduation, he knew he had chosen well. First there was the training at Fort Sill, followed by Artillery Basic. Along the way he got help for his dyslexia, and it was then that he began to expand his goals. He went to Ranger School and joined the famed 82nd Airborne at Fort Bragg. When he landed in the 310 Field Artillery, he knew he had found a home.

All this led to an assignment in Afghanistan. It seemed almost natural, somehow a part of family tradition. Russell's father, Joe, had been a Ranger in Vietnam, and his uncles fought in World War II and Korea. An early American Rippetoe had even fought under George Washington. Afghanistan was simply the next stage in the family calling.

During his three months in the country, Russell grew. He spent his down time playing soccer, wrestling with his buddies, and reveling in the ways of soldiers. And there was something else. He saw men die for the first time. It changed him. He pressed into his Christian roots, prayed often with his chaplain, and found a new passion for the Bible.

Somewhere along the way, someone gave him something that looked like his dog tag. It was called a

Shield of Strength. On one side there was a picture of the American flag with the words "One Nation Under God," and on the other were the modified words of Joshua 1:9: "I will be strong and courageous. I will not be terrified, or discouraged; for the Lord my God is with me wherever I go." Russell carried the Shield of Strength with him and soon learned that thousands of his fellow soldiers did likewise. It was an inspiration to confidence in God, a seal of martial unity through faith.

That faith went with him into Iraq. With his Shield of Strength around his neck and his ever present Bible— the camouflage-covered one with "Ranger 3rd Battalion" printed on it—in his backpack, Captain Rippetoe led his men through the early days of the Iraqi conflict. This is how he came to be near the strategic dam on April 3, 2003.

It was on that day that three white Suburbans pulled up to the checkpoint. Rippetoe and his men eyed them carefully. Suddenly, an excited, screaming woman jumped from the backseat of one of the vehicles. "I'm hungry. I need food and water," she cried. Rippetoe, always concerned for the safety of his men, ordered everyone to "hold back" and began walking toward the woman to see how he could help. When the woman saw him drawing near, she hesitated. It must have been the signal. The driver of one of the white Suburbans then detonated a bomb that blew a house-sized hole in the earth. Captain Russell Rippetoe and two of his men, Livaudais and Long, were killed. Others, wounded, survived to tell the tale of their captain's greatness.

Then began the grieving—and the haunting sense of destiny. When Capt. Rippetoe's father went to Fort Benning, Georgia, to collect his son's belongings, there was a note from the young officer attached to his wall locker. The simple, prophetic words betrayed the truth that Russell had known even before leaving for Iraq that he would never go home again. "I want a military funeral," he had written, "and I want it to be with my people."

And so it was. On the tenth of April, 2003, Captain Russell Rippetoe became the first American from the war in Iraq to be buried at Arlington National Cemetery. He was attended in death by his family and his fellow Rangers—the ones he had called "his people." And there were medals. The Army Rangers presented Captain Rippetoe's stricken parents with his two Bronze Stars for valor and a Purple Heart. There was also the American flag, the one from their son's coffin.

A few months later, President Bush honored Captain Rippetoe in his May 26 Memorial Day speech. After quoting the words of Joshua 1:9 from the slain man's Shield of Strength, the president then said, "This faithful Army captain has joined a noble company of service and sacrifice gathered row by row. These men and women were strong and courageous and not dismayed. And we pray they have found their peace in the arms of God."[1]

It is a story that seems destined to live on. At the Smithsonian Museum in Washington DC, there is an exhibit that includes the personal effects of Captain Rippetoe. Visitors to the museum can see the Ranger's gear—his helmet, goggles, web gear, boots, and uniform. These are no surprise. But then there are the symbols of the heart. Also on display is Rippetoe's Bible—the one with Ranger 3rd Battalion on it and the Ranger slogan: "Rangers Lead the Way." There is also a small cross, a second Bible, the captain's dog tags, and a small piece of metal that was scorched in the explosion that took the man's life. It is the Shield of Strength, the words of Joshua 1:9 still clear.

Now in his seventies and in the evening of his life, Russell Rippetoe's father often returns to Arlington to visit his son's grave—Number 7860, Section 60.[2] When he does, he never finishes his vigil without leaving one of the Shields of Strength atop his son's stone marker. It is an act that honors his son and reminds other visitors of the passion that gave his son's life meaning. The young man's father knows that now hundreds of thousands of the little shields have gone out into the world and that Rangers the world over carry them to honor their God and their fallen comrades.

They carry the little shields, too, so that faith will rise in their own hearts. The words they carry are taken from the words of God to Joshua when he was just about to enter the promised land of his day. Now, centuries later, soldiers strive to enter the promised land of their own destiny and of their national purpose. As they do, they are often reciting—in the barrens of Afghanistan, the rocky crags of Iraq—the meditation of an ancient warrior: "I will be strong and courageous. I will not be terrified, or discouraged; for the Lord my God is with me wherever I go."

Captain Russell Rippetoe's story possesses a blend of themes that have emerged from battlefields for generations and the style of a new generation at war. The ancient thread running through his tale is easy to see. He was an idealistic young officer who wanted to serve his country's cause but test his own mettle along the way. When confronted with hardship and death, he drank from the wells of faith his early religious training had dug for him. He prayed, studied, and celebrated his faith with others in the few moments of devotion that war allowed him. Then, while attempting to serve a people not his own, he died and was grieved by his family, lauded by his president, and given an honored place to rest in the capital of his country.

Most of these themes are as old as Homer and common to every war. Yet there is much that speaks of the new in Rippetoe's story. The passionate informality of the faith he found in the field is typical of his younger tribe at war. Moreover, this faith was inspired, in part, by a tiny Shield of Strength then popular among his fellow Rangers. It is almost the classic Millennial military icon: fashioned by a professional athlete who preaches "Xtreme Faith," sold on a website—www

.shieldsofstrength.com—and made, upon Rippetoe's death, a symbol of valor for a new generation that has now reached millions. There is one in the Oval Office, others in the pockets of congressmen and senators, and, aside from the official insignias they wear, it is the emblem most often carried by members of the military in Afghanistan and Iraq.

The popularity of the Shields of Strength may well be part of an attempt by Millennials to apply their faith, however informal it may be, to the demands of armed conflict. Every faith fashions some kind of code when it marches off to war. Millennial faith will be no different. It too will evolve a set of martial values, a corresponding code of ethics, slogans, and symbols. It too will guide the fighting of the young. Yet what will it produce? That question can only be answered—if it can be answered at all—after a look at the life of faith American soldiers are living as they fight their nation's battles abroad.

Adorning the walls of the dining facility—the DFAC—at Camp Victory in Iraq are posters that explain some of the world's great religions. The intended message is clear: "This is how a democracy deals with religion. It honors them all." Thus, above the heads of dining soldiers are brightly colored posters that depict the history and teachings of Christianity, Judaism, Buddhism, and Hinduism. Even Paganism and Wicca get their due. Nearly in the middle of them all is a poster extolling Islam. A soldier sitting nearby stares at it in surprise and mutters, "I wonder if Osama has seen this."

Though traditionally the military has thought in terms of "Protestant, Catholic, Jew," old religions of new strength in American culture have begun emerging among soldiers in Afghanistan and Iraq. Wiccans, neo-Pagans, Druids, and "servants of the Goddess" are now as vibrant if not as numerous as the Baptists in the field. There have been Native American powwows and New Age convergences and Hindu offerings in the

49

tents and trailers of American camps. The pantheon of American faiths is on display among soldiers overseas, and so long as a warrior's faith does not interfere with his duties or infringe on the rights of his comrades, his devotion is protected by military policy no matter how out of the mainstream it may be.

Of the greater world religions exerting new influence among soldiers, Buddhism is certainly in the lead, testament to the increasing numbers of Asians in the American military and to the appeal that Buddhism has among the young. With pop icons like Tina Turner, Richard Gere, and NBA coach Phil Jackson publicly converting to Buddhism, movies like *Seven Years in Tibet* encouraging its themes, and the engaging figure of the Dalai Lama as its most prominent spokesman, Buddhism has achieved its greatest foothold in American culture among the Millennials. More than once the Old Guard at Arlington National Cemetery has stood in their traditional blue uniforms next to Buddhist monks, striking against the somber green fields in red and yellow garb, as an American Buddhist patriot has been laid to rest.

The smallest religious group to have official chaplains are Jewish soldiers. They comprise no more than 1 percent of all soldiers abroad and are tended by a handful of rabbis, but their presence is particularly poignant.

For many Jewish soldiers, it has been a moving experience to live their traditions in a land that is so deeply intertwined with the history of their faith. Some have read the *Torah* along the ancient path that Abraham used to travel from Ur of the Chaldees, now in southern Iraq, to the Promised Land. Many have celebrated the Feast of Purim, the ancient festival honoring the courage of Queen Esther, in the very region where that story first took place. In fact, so many sites of Jewish history lie within the borders of Iraq that some Jewish soldiers proudly claim that they are fighting for righteousness in "the other Holy Land."

There is little doubt that America's Jewish soldiers are at greater risk in Iraq and Afghanistan than are the members of any other faith. The version of Islam that enflames the resistance to American troops also enflames a fierce anti-Semitism. This is nothing new. When journalist Daniel Pearl was kidnapped in Pakistan in 2002, his captors forced him to admit his Jewish blood just before they slit his throat. During the Gulf War, American captives suffered the indignity of having their pants pulled down so their Iraqi interrogators could see if they were circumcised, apparently unaware that many non-Jews are circumcised in the West. Downed Marine pilot Captain Michael Berryman was horribly beaten by his captors and then repeatedly asked, "What is your religion?" "Baptist," Berryman would reply. "No, you are a Jew!" his captors screamed, continuing the beatings. Such concerns moved the Pentagon to begin using "Protestant B" instead of "Jewish" on the dog tags of Jewish soldiers.

There are no such concessions in the present war. Expecting a quick victory and refusing to assume violations of International Law, the Pentagon has urged care among its Jewish fighters but has not taken steps to hide their identify. Nor, apparently, have some of the Jewish soldiers in the field. More than one has had the Star of David tattooed on his arm. "If they want a fight, they've got one," one of them said. "My people have a lot of experience at this kind of thing, and we aren't going to hide who we are now."

Of the tens of thousands of soldiers in Iraq and Afghanistan, the vast majority are in some form Christian. Their diversity, though, is astonishing. From Roman Catholics to Pentecostals, from Orthodox believers to the myriad of largely African American denominations, Jesus Christ is worshiped in most every possible fashion. There are the passionately "born again" who come from conservative, Bible-focused churches in the states and the believers who have never taken up space in a church but came to faith in a twelve-step program or through a favorite television preacher or from a study of the Bible on their own. Though the largest single religious group is Catholic, the second largest are those who represent the Protestant mainstream: Presbyterian, Baptist, Church of Christ, Methodist, Disciples of Christ, Christian Church, Church of God, or any of hundreds variations on a theme.

When these diverse Christian tribes step into the war zone, though, they cease to think in terms of their distinctives but are pressed by need and passion into a common pursuit of God. This is in part due to the influence of the chaplains. The military chapel system deals with faith in its broadest outlines. Most military installations have services for Catholics, Protestants, and Jews. There is no consideration of subsets. Jews are Jews; not Orthodox, Conservative, or Reform. Protestants are one group and not the hundreds of options one can choose. And Catholics lay claim to most everyone who aligns with a "historic faith."

53

This means that official faith becomes generic, and this has its advantages. The fastest-growing churches back home are interdenominational gatherings that downplay doctrine and focus on good music, meaningful preaching, and small groups that meet to apply truth to life. The chaplains know this and increasingly try to broaden the appeal of their services to the new generation in their care. There are "contemporary services" with praise bands—some of the musicians borrowed from the Army band—and with sermons often given by soldiers who have a message to share. There are "Gospel services," which are largely African American but usually have whites in attendance who are looking for something more vibrant than the customary offering. Since a chaplain must attend every official service the military offers, it is not uncommon to find a white chaplain swaying to what he hopes is the beat of the black choir at the Gospel service. His seminary training often fails him at moments like these.

There are, of course, the more traditional military chapels. These are scheduled at the traditional times and tend to be the better attended. The higher ranks attend these services, and it is at these that the style most approximates the mainline denominations at home. While the Catholic service retains its liturgical distinctiveness, the Protestant service is usually a generic, lightly liturgical affair that tends to take on the denominational flavor of the chaplain who is in charge.

It would be easy to diminish these attempts at formal faith in the field. Many have tried. In a scene from Francis Ford Coppola's *Apocalypse Now*, a chaplain depicted during the Vietnam War attempts to offer prayer near a makeshift altar and before a kneeling band of soldiers. Suddenly, a cow that is being airlifted by a helicopter releases his bowels and defecates from aloft on the altar and the chaplain. The message is clear: "War desecrates faith." The truth is, though, that war summons faith, and its altar of expression is often the heartfelt offering of the chaplain in the field, as we shall see in the next chapter.

Try as the chaplain might, though, he is fortunate if his services reach a small percentage of the total number of soldiers in his care. This is not entirely due to the spiritual preferences of the new generation at war. There is also the issue of time. In Iraq and Afghanistan at this writing, soldiers are working seven days a week. Chapel attendance, even when it is valued, routinely falls in priority to the pressing needs of war. There is also the chapel itself. Facilities for weekly religious services are in short supply. Space is limited, and some have suggested that this is by design. A large gathering of soldiers at a set time each week is too tempting a target for insurgents with rockets or mortars. Perhaps as important is the fact that many of the soldiers do not practice their faith by church attendance at home and have no intention of starting in the often less inviting atmosphere of a military chapel.

Yet chapel attendance is a flawed barometer of faith in the roiling world of a military camp. If faith is to be measured by a nose count at official chapel services, the conclusion has to be that religion holds little sway on America's modern warriors. Nothing could be further from the truth. In fact, the influence of faith among soldiers at war today rivals that of any American war. That faith, as we have seen, is of a new and nontraditional variety. Yet it is no less heartfelt, no less influential in the lives of soldiers. Indeed it may be that this new brand of faith, fed as it is by small groups and technology, is more effective in meeting the needs of soldiers than traditional chapel services are or even can be.

The search for faith in the American camps in Afghanistan and Iraq quickly arrives at the extensive networking of small groups that feed spirituality in war. Though sometimes as small as two or three soldiers, these miniature churches—these bands of brothers and sisters—sustain the life of the spirit most effectively. There are Bible studies, prayer groups, "accountability groups," book clubs, twelve-step meetings, and gatherings devoted to working through material from most every denomination and major Christian ministry in the states. Often these groups are defined by little more than an informal covenant among soldiers who do spiritual growth "on the fly": a tank crew quotes aloud the scriptures they have agreed to memorize or a band of military police about to go on duty discuss each other's needs so they can pray throughout the day. Whatever the purpose and whatever the design, the small-group networking of the Millennials clearly are the cells of the soldier's body of faith.

When these cells are energized by technology, faith burrows even more deeply into their lives. A walk through one of the camps in Iraq on a Sunday afternoon is a case in point. In one tent is a gathering of soldiers before a mini-DVD player. They are watching the influential African American preacher T. D. Jakes on a DVD his ministry makes available to servicemen free of charge. In a trailer down the row are four soldiers discussing C. S. Lewis's *Mere Christianity*. They acquired the book from a project called Books for Soldiers. All four of these soldiers simply logged on to www.booksforsoldiers.com from the computers provided in camp, requested Lewis's classic, and began their study group when the books arrived, a gift from publishers and private donations in the states.

Another soldier walking with an iPod is listening to a sermon from his home church that was preached only hours before. The church's technician attaches digital recordings of the Sunday morning service to e-mails that reach this soldier in the field before the faithful at home have finished eating lunch.

57

Certainly the most influential guide to faith among soldiers, other than the Bible, is Rick Warren's *The Purpose-Driven Life*. At home, the book is an astonishing success, having sold almost thirty million copies and broken nearly every record for books of its kind. It is not surprising that it would surface among soldiers overseas. Yet what has made the book so influential among servicemen and women is a combination of generosity and technology. Warren and his publisher made provision for thousands of copies of the book and an accompanying study guide to be sent to chaplains in Afghanistan and Iraq. Now *The Purpose-Driven Life* study groups take place in tents, beside Bradley Fighting Vehicles, and over tables at the DFAC. The book on tape is passed from CD player to notebook computer to iPod and sometimes even to the speaker system—the "Charlie Box"—of a Humvee on patrol.

Other books receive similar attention. There are groups that meet to discuss Dan Brown's *The Da Vinci Code*, another publishing phenomenon in the states, which, though fiction, is so laden with religious implications that more than a dozen nonfiction counter-books have hit the market. Soldiers in the field debate the book, download articles pro and con from websites, and return home to astonish their parents with their new knowledge of church history and art. Another often-seen treatment of religion is this author's *The Faith of George W. Bush*, which, again because of the good graces of a publisher, has been sent by the thousands to soldiers in the field.

Clearly, due to the press of war and the religious preferences of a new generation, for many Millennials informal community has replaced chapels, comrades have replaced chaplains, and technology has replaced liturgy. Yet it is also true that experience has replaced doctrine, and this raises the question of the thinking, the philosophy—perhaps the theology—that soldiers are evolving in the field. What is that combination of belief and practice that the religious networking of the Millennials is producing? If the new kind of soldier is keeping only what he finds usable, only "what works" of traditional faith, what does he still have in hand when everything else has been tested and found wanting?

What clearly does not "work," what does not survive the crucible of war, is a simplistic, one-answer-fits-all kind of spirituality. In fact, this is normally the first thing soldiers and their chaplains mention. "The soldier who has an easy religious answer for everything is the one I watch carefully," one commander said. "If a soldier doesn't have enough flex in his thinking, if his religion is a rigid set of unchangeable explanations for everything that happens in the world, then war is going to mess with his mind in a serious way."

Sometimes this "easy believism" leads to tragic results. One young soldier who newly joined a transportation company came fresh to the field with what some who served with him called a "happy faith." Bad things didn't happen to good people, this soldier believed. His church background taught him that the holy are protected from all harm and that his fellow soldiers suffered because they did not pray properly or live "the God kind of life." Some early successes only made this soldier bolder, both in the fight and in faith. Then, a female soldier this young man had become fond of was killed at his side.

The experience shook the inner workings of his soul, and, when he had no frame of reference for the experience, he began to unravel. Months went by, and his downward spiral grew more dramatic. Chaplains and counselors could not lift him out of the darkness that descended on him. When others in his company were killed, he sank deeper. The look of utter dislocation on his face became painful for his fellow soldiers to see. Nine months after arriving in country, this soldier—who had once been so bright and sure—opened a vein and bled himself to death.

"There is too much uncertainty in our world for simplistic thinking," one chaplain explained. "One man gets hit, and another right next to him survives. One vehicle rolls over an IED (Improvised Explosive Device), and nothing happens. The vehicle following gets demolished. Over here you have to have a sense of mystery—for a Christian, it would be the sovereignty of God—to survive in your mind. Any idea that certain things always happen or that certain things never happen will not only make a bad soldier but also is evidence of a flawed faith. A religion like this is the enemy of a good fighter."

What seems to be the friend of the fighter is the relational side of faith: the presence of God, the nearness of Jesus, the immanence of Jehovah, the light of Allah. Beliefs are important to the soldier in the field but only so far as they frame experience. Even for the theologically aware, the focus during crisis becomes simply, "Is God with me?" One chaplain approached a soldier who was preparing for a convoy down Route Irish, a contested route just outside of Baghdad known to be among the most dangerous stretches of road in the world. "What do you want?" the chaplain asked, meaning, "How can I minister to you?"

Without taking his eyes from his gear, the soldier said what for some has become the soldier's prayer:

"What do I want? Sir, I wanna' know that Jesus is in my Humvee."

This hunger for God's nearness is both a hope for protection and a need to answer the loneliness in a soldier's soul. Human beings face fear and death alone. But the soul is solitary, and the experience is personal. Even though a soldier may love his friends in arms, he knows they cannot fully protect him in battle or from the trauma that war brings to his soul. He needs God near and involved. This is why one chaplain said that his favorite name for God, and one he teaches his soldiers, is *"Emmanuel*—God with us."

To assure this nearness of God, to nail down the divine presence, soldiers turn to rituals. This is more than mere superstition. It is the human need for liturgy, for ceremonies of faith—however informal—that mark the defining moments of life. Hundreds of times a day soldiers in Afghanistan and Iraq band together before launching into their assigned duties to pray, say a blessing, recite a confession, or in some way immerse themselves in divine grace. Outside of Duhok in Northern Iraq, a band of Marines recites the Lord's Prayer together, their gloved hands stacked on top of one another like a football team before kickoff. At Camp Liberty, a female Hispanic sergeant makes the sign of the cross over a Humvee. Nearby, another Humvee driver waits for her to bless his vehicle. He is Baptist. His pastor at home would be appalled. He doesn't care. His sergeant is a deep woman of faith, and every vehicle she blesses comes back safely.

Rituals sometimes emerge in crisis when they never would at leisure. Kathleen Burke, a physician's assistant at the Camp Seitz medical clinic, says she is an agnostic but freely admits that she sometimes prays the Hail Mary when a friend is wounded or someone is dying under her care. "You hang on to what you're taught," she explains. "Sometimes the words come when you don't intend it. You'll use anything that works, even if you're embarrassed by it later."

What drives much of a soldier's religion in the field, particularly these rituals he employs, is the urge to access spiritual power. Bands of soldiers memorize scriptures together, for example, to wring from the words the needed comfort, peace, or strength. It is not uncommon to find Humvees filled with a majority of Christians playing throbbing worship music on the sound system "so that God will inhabit the praise of His people." Medics report that they sometimes have to push away friends of a fallen comrade who insist on laying hands on the wounded and asking God for healing.

This is very much in keeping with the Millennials' passion for a working, experience-oriented, "real" religion. One soldier who came to the field a self-described atheist reported, "I haven't had a change so much in philosophy as I have in experience. I never decided to believe in God over here. I just wanted to survive. I joined the other guys when they prayed or blessed themselves because I thought they had a power I didn't have. Then I seemed to have it, too. That power had to come from somewhere, so I guess I'm not an atheist anymore."

A final element of the newly fashioned religious philosophy of the Millennials is the power of story. Scholars have long spoken of the postmodernism of the new generation, of their disbelief in comprehensive worldviews—Christianity, Marxism, Islam—but of their belief in stories and myths, which create the reality of a tribe. Some see this simply as the conditioning of a media age. A scene from a movie provides a better point of reference for Millennials than words from the Bible or ideas from the great thinkers. Images and stories replace words and ideas. These stories become the stuff of faith and define belief far more than systematic truth.

When most soldiers are asked why they fight in Iraq and Afghanistan, they don't reply with ideals but with images of September 11, 2001, and their own family's experience. When the president prays with a wounded soldier at Walter Reed Hospital and kisses him after pinning on a metal, the tale circulates through the military and does more good than a hundred speeches. And when soldiers are pressed by reporters about whether their presence means good for the countries they have liberated, soldiers normally respond with stories about cheering crowds of Iraqis or women who can now read in Afghanistan. The story, the narrative, is the expression of truth.

To talk with young soldiers in the field today is to hear grief, faith, fear, and vision expressed in terms of story. Sergeant Brett Pyles is a medic at the Troop Medical Clinic of Camp Victory. His ability to enter the story of the soldiers who die under his care has pressed him to a deeper level of faith. "When a man dies, it is my job to take out his wallet and handle his paperwork," Pyles relates softly. "I look at the pictures he has—of his wife or his kids or his parents—and I realize they don't know yet. They think he is still alive. They're somewhere praying for him and waiting for him to come home. But he's dead. That's the hardest moment for me. It breaks my heart, and it makes me realize that I can die, too. Life can be taken away in a second. I find myself even praying on my way to the toilet. I want to live, but I want to be ready when I die even more."

This passion for stories that give hope and define faith has caused some tales emerging from the war to

65

achieve almost legendary status. One Christmas morning, a man named only "Sgt. C" in the press was leading an assault squad to clean out a nest of insurgents in Baghdad. Small arms fire broke out, and Sgt. C decided to round a corner and take stock of the situation he and his men were in. As he did, he found himself looking into the barrel of a 9mm automatic pistol. Before the sergeant could react, the Iraqi holding the pistol pulled the trigger. Though he remembered thinking he was about to die, the sergeant found himself still standing. Assuming the gun had misfired, he immediately advanced on the Iraqi who, now in shock himself, instantly surrendered.

After the mission was complete, Sgt. C. began feeling light-headed. Urged to go to the hospital, he arrived covered in blood and soon realized his front tooth was missing. He assumed the ballistic shock from the Iraqi's pistol had knocked it loose. He was wrong. X-rays revealed that the Iraqi's gun had not misfired but had instead implanted a bullet exactly where the missing tooth had been. The bullet had apparently entered Sgt. C just below his nose and then positioned itself in place of the missing tooth, what dentists call "the apex of #8." This story was widely circulated by e-mail in the American camps and at home and was told in the *Army Times*. It became a lesson of God's grace for those who trust Him. Pinned on bulletin boards and folded into helmets, the story became an inspiration to faith for thousands.

The faith of the Millennials at war, then, is nurtured by informal community rather than by traditional structures and is geared toward flexible beliefs that center around the presence of God, rituals of divine blessing, access to power, and stories that inspire and inform. Yet does this new brand of faith have any meaning for how soldiers fight? Is there an ethic for soldiers to be found in what Millennials believe?

The disconcerting truth is that the faith of the Millennials is so diverse and so informal that while it does frame a warrior ethic, it does so in inconsistent and even conflicting ways. This is so much so that it cannot be relied upon to guide the conduct of warriors in any meaningful way.

Part of the reason for this failure on the part of Millennial faith is that it is, by definition, personal and tribal. It does not intend to have answers for the world as a whole. It intends to provide meaningful experience for the individual. This is the legacy that postmodernism has left for Millennial faith. The new generation does not think in terms of what is true, but in terms of "what is true for me." Faith and truth are personal, limited to "my group," and not expected to be equally meaningful for the world as a whole.

The other reasons that Millennial faith is an inconsistent guide for warriors is the very diversity that is its strength. Two stories, admittedly extreme, illustrate the point. Sergeant Brett Barry came to faith under the influence of fellow soldiers in Iraq. These soldiers are from a large church in San Antonio, Texas, where the nationally known preacher speaks often on the evils of Islam. According to this pastor, Muhammad was a demon-possessed man, Islam is an anti-Christ religion, and the Quran calls on Muslims to ultimately immerse the world in a bloodbath. Sgt. Barry is but a few months old in his faith, but he is already convinced that the battles he fights in Iraq are with a system of spiritual evil that must be confronted both with prayer and military might.

The problem is that Sgt. Barry is becoming less concerned about the death of civilians, less careful about what the military calls "collateral damage." He is not fighting terrorists; he is fighting a religious system, because the faith he learned in a tent full of soldiers tells him that system is a source of the world's evil. So the faith he found in informal community and that is shaped by stories about Islam is framing his conduct in war. Yet, his faith is not making him the warrior the U.S. military hopes to put in the field. It is making him dangerous or, as one of his non-Christian fellow soldiers has said, "His faith is making him another Abu Ghraib waiting to happen."

By contrast, Corporal Angela Lynn is moving in a different direction. She was what she describes as a "nominal Catholic" until she went to Iraq and was almost killed in the bombing of the DFAC in Mosul late in 2004. To get through the trauma of that event, she leaned on the wisdom and kindness of a Catholic chaplain and found herself deepening in her devotion to her faith. She joined a group of Catholic soldiers who were reading the mystical literature of the church—calling themselves the "Dead Catholics Society"—and began moving toward a mystical faith that came very close to pacifism. She has now decided that she has no intention of killing another human being. She will serve out her tour of duty and then become a nun, but she has determined she will never fire her weapon again.

69

Corporal Lynn has made a personal theological choice that neither the military chaplain who got her through her crisis nor the soldiers who read the mystics with her know about. Her decision is deeply religious, deeply at odds with her military role, and deeply dangerous. Her commanders assume she will stand her post and fire when ordered. But she says privately that she will not, and lives will be risked. In her homespun pacifism, she is perhaps as dangerous as Sgt. Barry. Both have made decisions at odds with Army doctrine. Both put lives at risk. Both are allowing their personal faith to influence their military role to the detriment of their country.

The additional problem is that the military is not permitted to address the conduct of the war at a religious level. True, there are Soldier's Creeds and formalized military values that are preached to soldiers throughout their careers, as we shall see. The enemy is often referred to as "the bad guys," and the evils of terrorism are lightly addressed in training for those who might have missed the lesson on September 11, 2001. Yet this is as far as it goes. The nature of radical Islam, the righteousness of the war, the religious implications of killing, the spiritual justification of the American cause—these cannot be addressed by a religiously neutral American military. This means that the highly individualistic, informal theologies that Millennials fashion fill the vacuum left by a religiously silent military culture. No unified warrior code triumphs. Instead, a variety of warrior codes arise as informal faiths create them, leaving an unevenness if not an inconsistency to the conduct of warriors in the field.

Obviously, several significant trends are on a collision course: the informal but passionately held religions of the Millennials, the likelihood that for years to come America's primary enemy in the world will be a religious network, and the increasing demand for religious neutrality on the part of the American military, a trend we will consider in the next chapter. And at the convergence of them all is the devoted but tragically hamstrung military chaplain.

A good chaplain does good like a hundred men. He makes us feel like God is with us and we can do anything if we have faith. A bad chaplain, though, almost makes you ashamed to be a soldier.

—A PRIVATE AT CAMP VICTORY
IN BAGHDAD, IRAQ

CHAPTER 3

MEN OF CLOTH AND STEEL

It was February 2, 1943, and the American transport ship *Dorchester* was steaming through the icy North Atlantic just off the coast of Greenland. The 902 soldiers she carried were tense. Everyone knew where they were—the dreaded "Torpedo Junction," where a hundred Allied merchant and marine ships a month were being sunk by torpedoes from German submarines. And Captain Hans J. Danielson knew something that most on board did not. His sonar readings indicated that an enemy sub was nearby.

To ease the stress and fear, the four military chaplains aboard scheduled an amateur night that filled the ship with the explosive laughter of men in need of relief. It was the kind of thing these chaplains did, for they were extraordinary men, as the night's events would soon reveal.

The eldest of them was George Fox. He was forty-two and could have easily avoided being on the *Dorchester* that night. He had already served his country well in the First World War. Convincing the recruiters that he was older than he was, Fox had joined the Army at the age of seventeen, served in the medical corps, and performed so courageously that he earned the Silver Star, the Croix de Guerre, and the Purple Heart. By the outbreak of World War II, he was a Methodist minister who could have stayed with his congregation at home. Instead, he told his family, "I've got to go. I know from experience what our boys are about to face. They need me."[1]

The youngest of the four chaplains aboard the *Dorchester* was Clark Poling. A Dutch Reformed pastor, he had rejected the idea of serving as a chaplain when the war began. "I'm not going to hide behind the church in some safe office out of the firing line," he roared at his father one night. His father had been a chaplain in World War I and understood. "Don't you know," he told his son, "that chaplains have the highest mortality rate of all? As a chaplain you'll have the best chance in the world to be killed. You just can't carry a gun to kill anyone yourself." Satisfied he wasn't taking the coward's way, Clark Poling went to war.

Alexander Goode, the third chaplain on the *Dorchester*, had followed in the rabbinic calling of his father. He was already in the National Guard when the clouds of war began to form and, ten months before Pearl Harbor, tried to become a Navy chaplain. The Navy had rejected him, but when war actually came, Goode was desperate to serve his nation in the troubled times that were sure to come. Finally, he gained entrance as an Army chaplain and never looked back.

The only Catholic among the four chaplains was John P. Washington. He was a small man who wore glasses and seemed more the bookish, artistic type. But growing up one of nine children in a raucous Irish family and living on the streets in the toughest part of Newark, Washington acquired a fierceness that his body didn't betray. When war broke out, he was the beloved priest of the New Jersey streets. Before long, though, he had put his blend of piety and grit in the service of his God as a chaplain in the Army.

The four had met at the chaplain's school that was based for a while at Harvard University. Though religiously diverse, they became close friends and often prayed together in a way that astonished their fellow ministers. This bonding gave them a familiarity with each other's religion that served them well. It was not uncommon for a Catholic soldier to call for a chaplain and find Rabbi Goode at his side reciting the *Hail Mary* or the *Our Father*.

It was this love and friendship that had sustained these four and carried them to that chilly night aboard the *Dorchester* on February 3, 1943. Aware of looming danger, Captain Danielson had ordered everyone to sleep in their life jackets. The lower decks were steamy with the press of bodies though, and most aboard disobeyed. Then it happened. A loud explosion rocked the ship and sent the men into panic. The German submarine U-233 had scored a direct hit below the waterline. The *Dorchester* was going down. The order to abandon ship was given.

The four chaplains spread out among the soldiers and began caring for the injured, praying with the dying, and guiding the men into lifeboats. Petty Officer John J. Mahoney tried to go below to get his gloves, but

Rabbi Goode stopped him. "Here, take these," Goode insisted, when he found out what Mahoney was after. "I have two pair." Mahoney suspected it wasn't true, that the rabbi probably did not have a second pair. Gratefully, though, he took the gift.

Soon the *Dorchester* began to slip into the sea. When all lifeboats were launched and all life jackets were gone, men began to realize their situation—soldiers were going to die. Without hesitation, the four chaplains took off their life jackets and gave them to those who had none. Then, finding each other in the dark, the four men of God linked arms, grasped the railing of the ship together, and began shouting encouragement to the men in the sea.

"It was," said John Ladd, a survivor, "the finest thing I have seen or hope to see this side of heaven." Above the moans and cries of grief, soldiers in the lifeboats or floating in the water could hear their four chaplains singing and shouting encouragement together. First they heard the Lord's Prayer in English. Then they heard all four men—the Protestants, the Catholic, and the Jew—calling out the *Shema* in Hebrew: "Hear, O Israel, the Lord thy God, the Lord thy God is one"—"*Shema Yisroel, Adonai Ehohainu, Adonai Echod.*" Latin was next, with Father Washington leading the way in portions of the Catholic Mass. When all this was done, the chaplains would preach faith in God to their perishing men and then return to the ancient words of comfort from all their faiths. Private First Class William Bednar, floating among his dead comrades, later said, "Their voices were the only thing that kept me going."

Finally, twenty-seven minutes after the torpedo hit, the *Dorchester* slipped beneath the waves, taking the four chaplains to their deaths in the deep. Only 230 men survived the day. One of them was John Mahoney, the man who had taken the gloves offered by Rabbi Goode. Once the *Dorchester* went down, Mahoney spent eight hours at the oars of a lifeboat fighting the towering waves that threatened to wash him overboard. "Those gloves," he remembered years later, "saved my life."

Just before boarding the *Dorchester*, Clark Poling had written his father, the former World War I chaplain, and told him how to pray: "Not for my safe return, that wouldn't be fair. Just pray that I shall do my duty...never be a coward...and have the strength, courage, and understanding of men. Just pray that I shall be adequate."[2]

Today when visitors walk through the memorial chapel at the Pentagon or pray in the Community Chapel at West Point, they can look up and see the *Dorchester* chaplains commemorated in beautiful stained glass windows that celebrate the heroism of Washington,

Fox, Poling, and Goode. Each year the Immortal Chaplains Foundation gives an award for heroism called the *Immortal Chaplains Prize for Humanity*. It is given in memory of the *Dorchester*'s "immortal four."

The tale of the *Dorchester* chaplains captures the best of what a military chaplain strives to be. In their self-sacrifice, their broad-mindedness, their spiritual passion, and their devotion to their troops, these chaplains embodied the highest that men of God in war have hoped to achieve and set a vision of greatness for future generations. They symbolize the dream, and it is the ministers in uniform on battlefields today who carry that dream in their hearts.

America's military chaplains occupy what must surely be among the most unique positions in the world. Theirs is a universe of contradictions. They are a holdover from an earlier age of faith, much like congressional chaplains or the words "In God We Trust" on American coins or religious inscriptions on the official buildings in the nation's capitol. Clearly, the modern understanding of the First Amendment would never have given them birth. Yet the religious nature of their nation's enemy, the moral crises of America's soldiers, and the spiritual passions of the new generation at war may make them more essential to America's military efforts today than ever before.

The inconsistencies do not stop there. They wear a uniform but cannot carry a weapon. They receive a check from the state to do the work of the church in a society deathly afraid of the mixture of church and state. They can preach God's will for the individual soul but may not preach God's will for the war. They are ordained by a single religious denomination to preach its truth but as chaplains must tend every possible religious persuasion.

The religious nature of their calling often works against them. If a chaplain is deployed with his National Guard unit, every man he serves is guaranteed a job to come home to. Yet if that chaplain was a pastor in a church when he was sent off to war, he is not guaranteed he can return to his job. The government he serves cannot pressure a church to employ that chaplain again. It is a violation of the separation of church and state.

He is supposed to tend the needs of soldiers at war. Yet he is not supposed to get too close to the fighting. The military is concerned that if a chaplain accompanies soldiers into battle, the soldiers will be distracted from their mission out of concern for the safety of the chaplain, whom they often love and who is required to be unarmed. Yet the biggest complaint about chaplains from soldiers in the field is that they "don't cross the wire with us, and so they don't know how we feel."

Then there is the chain of command. Pastors fighting with deacons and church boards is such a common occurrence back home that there are courses on the subject in seminaries. Yet a chaplain in the military can end up working for a commander who thinks all faith is silly or who views the particular religion of the chaplain as heresy. One battalion commander was disciplined for calling his Catholic chaplain, a Major Pappas, by the nickname "Major Papist," a denigrating reference to the myth that Catholics worship the pope. Another chaplain was told by his executive officer, "Be as religious as you want to be, but stay away from me and my troops." Church fights at home pale in comparison to these pressures.

Adding to these contradictions and challenges are the "knuckleheads in clerical garb" who taint the image of the role. There is the overheated evangelist who offends more than he wins, the office rat who does ministry only behind a desk, the one the troops call "Captain Kangaroo" who hands out candy but nothing more as men go off to battle, the "cheerleader" whose every sermon sounds like a pitch from an Army recruiter, and the bulbous gourmand who couldn't pass the Army physical fitness test unless he hired someone

81

to take it for him. Each of these leaves legacies for other chaplains to live down.

Yet despite the oddities and obstacles of their role, chaplains are often among the noblest figures in the field. There is the stunning bravery of a chaplain risking enemy fire to give Last Rites to a dying man. There are the highly decorated fighting men who have then gone on to seminary so they can return to the service and minister to men in arms. And there are the noble dead among the chaplains' corps who, like the *Dorchester* chaplains, lost their lives tending the warrior soul.

In fact, many of these chaplains are models of toughness. Colonel Gene Fowler was the head chaplain in Iraq through 2003, serving in the 3rd Corps. A slight, bespectacled man, Chaplain Fowler has nevertheless proven his steel on more than one occasion. While serving as a chaplain at a stateside post, a grizzled master sergeant once approached him, looked him up and down, and said, "Sir, if you ain't Airborne, you ain't nothing." Refusing to let the challenge go unanswered and hating the thought that, once again, a clergyman should be viewed as a wimp, Chaplain Fowler went to Ranger school and became an honored member of the Airborne fraternity. Now he wears the Ranger tab and Airborne wings on his uniform, yet when he jumps from a plane, he does so without a weapon. He is there to fight battles of the spirit.

Chaplain Fowler and the hundreds of other chaplains who serve with him today stand in an honored tradition that reaches back through the centuries. The literature of the ancient world is filled with stories of priests leading the way in battle. It was a time when war between tribes was understood as a contest of gods. Sometimes the actual fighting would have to wait until each tribe's priest had adequately insulted the other tribe's god, for only then was it proper to attack.

The priests of Israel also played a role in war. The Book of Deuteronomy records the words that the priests were to say to Israel's warriors before battle. Sometimes the priest led the way. In the famous battle of Jericho, priests sounding rams' horns marched around that city for six days before the invasion began and the city was taken. Later in history, Roman armies depended on their priests to sacrifice the appropriate animals before battle and to read the entrails to discern whether victory was certain. It almost always was.

The modern chaplaincy, though, has its origins in the Middle Ages. According to *A Brief History of the United States Chaplains Corp*, the Council of Ratisbon first authorized chaplains for armies in A.D. 742, and the very word *chaplain* comes from this period. A Roman soldier named Martin of Tours once came upon a beggar shivering from the cold and gave him a part of his cloak. Later that same night, Martin had a vision of Christ dressed in the cloak and decided the next day to devote his life to the church. After his death, he was canonized and became the patron saint of France. His cloak, now a holy relic, was carried into battle by the Frankish kings. The cloak itself was called by its Latin name, the *cappa*. The portable shrine it was carried in was called the *capella*. The priest who tended the cloak and its shrine was called the *cappellanus*, and eventually all clergy in the military were called by that name, which in French is *chapelains* and in English *chaplains*.[3]

The colonial Americans put their touch on this European tradition with the rise of the *fighting parson*. Pastors in colonial villages often led militias drawn from their own congregations into battle against Indians or European enemies. The first of these—in fact, the first military chaplain on record in American history—was Reverend Samuel Stone of the Church of Christ in Hartford, Connecticut, who accompanied militias in the Pequot War of 1637. Often these warrior pastors were the fiercest fighters among their peers, shouting scriptures, urging courage, and calling down curses on the enemy, all while plunging boldly into a waiting foe.[4]

By the time of the American Revolution, these pastors had become the colonial combined equivalent of Billy Graham and George Patton. They were the fiercest Christians, the wisest counselors, and the first to serve a just cause in war. They embodied the warrior code of their generation. One memorable example of this breed was John Peter Muhlenberg. A thirty-year-old pastor and member of the Virginia House of Burgesses, Muhlenberg is best known for a sermon he preached on the eve of the Revolution. His text was Ecclesiastes 3:1: "To every thing there is a season, and a time to every purpose under the heaven." After developing his text, the pastor closed with these words: "In the language of the Holy Writ, there is a time for all things. There is a time to preach and a time to fight." At that point, Muhlenberg threw off his black preaching robe to reveal the uniform of a colonel in the 8th Virginia Regiment. That same afternoon, he led three hundred men, largely of his own congregation, to join General Washington's troops.[5]

85

Such fighting parsons were so valuable to the colonial cause that the Continental Congress gave chaplains their first official recognition on July 29, 1775, when it voted twenty dollars per month for men who would keep the gospel of God central in the fight. *A Brief History of the United States Chaplains Corp* relates that on July 9, 1776, after the Congress increased the pay for chaplains, George Washington issued the following General Order to his troops:

> The Honorable Continental Congress having been pleased to allow a Chaplain to each Regiment, with the pay of Thirty-three Dollars and one third dollars per month—The Colonels or commanding officers of each regiment are directed to procure Chaplains accordingly; persons of good Character and exemplary lives—To see that all inferior officers and soldiers pay them a suitable respect and attend carefully upon religious exercises. The blessing and protection of Heaven are at all times necessary but especially so in times of public distress and danger—The General hopes and trusts, that every officer and man, will endeavor so to live, and act as becomes a Christian Soldier defending the dearest Rights and Liberties of this country.[6]

This desire for the blessing of heaven and Christian soldiers to defend it was central to the thinking of the founding generation. Their understanding of the role of religion in the Republic was vastly different from that of today. What that generation feared was a state church, an official religion for the nation, like the Anglican Church of the England from which they had just separated. This was the meaning of the First Amendment: to prevent the federal government from establishing a state church and to assure that individuals could worship as they wished. What the founding generation did not fear was a central role for faith, primarily Christian faith, in the Republic. In fact, they doubted that the nation would survive without the "blessing of heaven."

The founding generation intertwined faith and government—though never the institutional church and government—in a way that would spin the minds of those seeking a radical separation of church and state today. Congress called for days of prayer and fasting, printed Bibles, funded Christian missionaries to the Indians, appointed congressional chaplains, and referenced faith in its political debates, all without the slightest thought that this might be a violation of the law. Presidents wrote freely of religion, preached in churches, invoked God's name in official proclamations, and knew they could not get elected unless they articulated their beliefs clearly.

Even the federal buildings in the new city of Washington DC were used as churches on weekends, and no objection was ever raised.

Therefore, as the new country was born, the idea that the nation must be faithful to God prevailed. It was natural, then, to want prayer, Scripture reading, religious teaching, and personal ministry connected with most every endeavor, from the proceedings of the Congress to the Army in the field. The military chaplain continued as part of this new order and preserved the tradition of the "fighting parson" in the new nation's armed forces.

Chaplains proved themselves in all of the wars that would soon follow, from the War of 1812 to the Mexican War, but it was the Civil War that would transform the chaplaincy most. It was this national catastrophe that witnessed the advent of the first Jewish chaplains, the first black and Indian chaplains, and the rise of the military chaplaincy to new heights of honor.

Indeed, it is not going too far to say that the work of chaplains may have changed the course of the war. After the first year of conflict, both Confederate and Union troops were mired in the depression and disillusionment that prolonged bloodshed brings. Chaplains began searching for a solution. Many of them considered resigning and returning home. In "Born Again in the Trenches: Revivals in the Army of Tennessee," G. Cinton Prim Jr. relates that by the winter of 1862–63, chaplains in General Braxton Bragg's command, for example, were so discouraged that they considered resigning en masse. But at a meeting to discuss the proposal, a Baptist minister, Reverend L. H. Millikan, offered three resolutions:

1. That the souls of the vast multitudes are too precious to be abandoned to perdition

2. That God is able to give His own called ministers the victory even among soldiers

3. That the chaplains should enter into a covenant to pray for each other, and that all should at once begin protracted meetings in their several regiments claiming this whole army for the King of kings[7]

Taking these words as a covenant among them, the ministers gave themselves immediately to prayer and began scheduling religious meetings. Within weeks each chaplain reported revivals in his regiment. As Prim reports in his article, one minister wrote in the *Southern*

Presbyterian of April 1863: "I have attended many revivals—have had several at my own church—but I have never seen one of such interest as this."[8] Indeed, before long the biggest problem the ministers had was a lack of help. Crying out for more chaplains and missionaries, one minister wrote that with more preachers, "I think we would have a great revival. I never saw men so anxious to hear preaching. They crowd around the preaching place two or three hours before the preacher gets there."[9] When the Army of Tennessee moved to Chattanooga, Reverend W. H. Browning reported, "There is now a general spirit of revival manifest in every part of the army." The Army seemed transformed: "Instead of oaths, jests, and the blackguard songs, one heard the songs of Zion, prayer, and praises of God." Instead of a "school of vice" the Army became "the place where God is adored, and where many learn to revere the name of Jesus."[10]

When Chaplains T. H. Davenport and John B. Chapman of the Twenty-sixth and Thirty-second Tennessee Regiments began a series of meetings, the results surprised even them. Their twenty-five-foot square meeting house had to be expanded to seventy-five by sixty feet to accommodate more than a thousand soldiers at a time. Soldiers assembled morning and night for three months. Davenport described the crowd he had the privilege of addressing.

> Every eye is on the speaker; not a head, hand or foot is seen moving, the big tears are stealing down their sunburnt cheeks. Mourners are called, and the large altar is crowded with weeping penitents. Those lion-hearted men who had so often faced dangers, and who would scorn to beg mercy of the foe, are at the feet of Jesus, humbly, earnestly begging pardon and mercy. . . . Nothing was done for vain glory; all were in earnest.[11]

Of another meeting one minister wrote, "Men who never shrank in battle from any responsibility came forward weeping. Such is the power of the Gospel of Christ when preached in its purity."[12] Dozens of similar meetings were held with thousands of lives changed. Some even felt the call to the ministry themselves, for as one chaplain wrote, "Strange as it may seem to many . . . the call to preach the gospel of Christ came to the hearts of the men of war on the tented field; and no sooner were their carnal weapons laid aside than they buckled on the Divine armor, and, seizing the sword of the Spirit entered the battle against the power of darkness."[13] As

91

the war neared an end, the revivals became symbols of what might happen in a better postwar America. The Presbyterians who gathered in Georgia in December of 1865 held tightly to just such a hope.

> That our camps should have been made nurseries of piety, is something not only new and unprecedented in warfare, but may be regarded as an encouraging token of God's purpose to favor and bless our future Zion. If these rich and spiritual gifts are carefully gathered and husbanded for the Master's use, we may soon have occasion to forget our temporal sorrows in the abundance of our spiritual joys.[14]

Revival spread among troops in both Union and Confederate Armies, but the forces of the South were most deeply affected. Some historians have claimed that the transforming nature of the revivals was so extensive that men lost their heart for fighting, and the war moved more rapidly to a close. However these revivals are interpreted, they propelled the military chaplaincy to new levels of influence during the Civil War. This new authority was also a result of the heroism many chaplains displayed. Three chaplains earned the Congressional Medal of Honor during the war, and many others were cited for bravery.

Chaplains continued to earn respect during the wars to win the American West and the Spanish-American War, which was the first war in which they accompanied troops overseas. One of these, Henry A. Brown, served with the "Rough Riders" of Theodore Roosevelt, who later said of Brown that he showed "great courage and humanity in succoring my wounded men under heavy fire."[15]

Chaplains continued to shine in the First World War, as well. In the horrors of trench warfare and the nightmarish collision of new weapons with old tactics, chaplains led worship during bombardments, risked artillery fire to tend the dying, and made themselves the embodiment of hope and courage. Ministry was ecumenical. A chaplain comforting dying soldiers might read a psalm to a Protestant, hold a crucifix to the lips of a Catholic, or lead a Jewish soldier in the Hebrew confession of faith. Several of these pastors of men at arms stood out. Francis P. Duffy, a Roman Catholic priest from New York, so inspired the men of the "Irish 69th" that his statue stands in New York's Times Square to this day. When Coleman E. O'Flaherty was awarded the Distinguished Service Cross (DSC) for his sacrifices, his commander said the letters actually stood for "Died in the Service of Christ."[16]

By the advent of World War II, the role of the chaplain was so widely recognized as essential to the fighting will of soldiers that in 1941 President Roosevelt signed Congressional Bill HR-3617, authorizing the construction of 604 chapels to nurture the spirits of that generation's warriors.[17] Knowing that strong faith made good fighters, General of the Army George Marshall devoted himself to assuring that the religious needs of soldiers were met. He ordered the construction of more than 550 cantonment chapels and assured that there were more than 9,111 chaplains—one for every 1,200 soldiers—in the Army and the Army Air Corps.[18]

During the Second World War, the chaplains' corps ballooned from a few hundred to nearly ten thousand. It was a revolutionary time for faith in uniform. More than half of the rabbis in America volunteered for the chaplaincy: two were killed in action, and forty-six were decorated for bravery. More than seven hundred ninety black chaplains served compared to only fifty-seven in World War I, and the first Buddhist chaplain might have served the 442nd Infantry, an all Japanese American unit, but Christian chaplains of Japanese descent were assigned instead.[19]

The war in Korea was the first American war against Communism and had a religious dimension as a result. The Communist forces of North Korea took pride in publicly persecuting missionaries and desecrating churches. They also subjected captured American chaplains to horrendous torture, and more than a few died in captivity. This was a terrible loss, both of an heroic life and because the chaplains' corps during the Korean War never numbered beyond 1,448—one for every 4,000 soldiers—far beneath the need.[20]

As it was for many facets of American life, the Vietnam War was a turning point for the American chaplaincy. The slogging jungle battles seemed to parallel a moral and spiritual depression at home that left the American soul devastated and the war in Vietnam largely without support among the American people. This meant a loss of resolve among churches, as well, and the effects on the chaplaincy are difficult to exaggerate. Chaplains are recommended for military service by their religious denominations. When many denominations in the United States lost faith in the American cause in Vietnam, they stopped sending chaplains, exacerbating the moral and spiritual crises among the troops. Drugs, racial tension, the lack of a moral rationale for the war, and the seeming unwillingness on the part of the nation's leaders to fight so as to win—all made the chaplain's challenge in Vietnam an overwhelming task.

In the years since Vietnam, the chaplaincy has been transformed—largely through the lessons learned during that troubled era. During the years of the war in Vietnam, the spiritual work of the chaplains had become purposely divorced from the behavior of men in the field. This was, in part, due to the increasing sense in society that religion was, at best, irrelevant to the "real world" and, at worst, destructive to personal freedom. In a culture built on such thinking, chaplains tended the heart of a man but seldom addressed his conduct in war. This divorce of faith and ethics, this weakening of chaplains as framers of the American warrior code, may have contributed to incidents like My Lai and the cheating scandals at West Point. In any case, the need for the "moral presence" of chaplains among troops came to be newly appreciated, and soon chaplains began to assume something closer to the roles they had held in earlier eras: the prophetic voice in the midst of soldiers and their fight. On the wings of this recovered understanding, chaplains began teaching ethics, serving as moral advisors to commanders, and speaking more freely of the connection between spirituality and martial conduct. Though chaplains have yet to return fully to the more traditional understanding of their role, they have at least broken with the spiritual legacy of Vietnam.

Perhaps as significant was the change that occurred in the way chaplains were chosen for military service. According to Dr. John Brinsfield, the senior historian for the Army Chaplains corps, chaplains had traditionally been chosen through a quota system in which the number of chaplains for a given denomination was determined by how many men and women in the service were from that denomination. Therefore, if 15 percent of servicemen and women were Baptists, for example, then 15 percent of the chaplains would be drawn from the Baptist denomination. It was an attempt to be fair and to serve the spiritual needs of soldiers, but it also meant that a qualified man in a given denomination might not be chosen if that denomination's quota was already filled. Instead, a less gifted man from another denomination might go in his place.

This system was replaced during the 1980s. Because fewer soldiers were affiliated with a religious denomination, and because many theologically and politically liberal denominations had seldom filled their quotas of chaplains since the years of the Vietnam War, the military began to choose chaplains on a "best qualified basis." This meant that the candidate with the best education, best civilian experience, best physical conditioning, and greatest likelihood of success in ministering to soldiers was chosen regardless of what his denomination was.

As Dr. Brinsfield—who wrote Field Manual 16-1, which ordered this change in policy—explains, "This not only gave the military a better quality of chaplain, but it also moved the chaplaincy as a whole in a more theologically conservative and even patriotic direction. The more liberal denominations had little vision for the military chaplaincy. They had moved theologically leftward in the years since the Vietnam War, and this had also left them a bit less patriotic, less interested in serving the military. When the 'best qualified' doctrine began, the denominations still sending chaplains were usually theologically conservative and strongly patriotic—such as the Southern Baptists, Pentecostals, the Churches of Christ, and so on. The chaplaincy as a whole was soon filled with highly qualified, theologically conservative men and women who saw it as a privilege to serve God by serving their nation."

It was a change in policy that transformed the chaplains' corps. Men and women held the job not because they were assigned by their denominations or because conditions were better for them in the service than their gifts would have earned for them in civilian ministry. They went into the chaplaincy—as many had before, but not all—with a sense of calling and with a passion to impact soldiers. They surrendered the better pay and perhaps the greater esteem of civilian ministry, and they moved their families around the world to serve their God in the lives of soldiers, airmen, sailors, and Marines.

Today, the American chaplains' corps is as fine as the nation has ever put in the field. Each chaplain has joined the military voluntarily. Each is well educated. Most are deeply devoted to those they serve and now see their ministry in a post-9/11 world as a vital service to their nation and their God. In Afghanistan and Iraq, hundreds of chaplains subject themselves to life-threatening dangers.

Yet the military chaplain serves in a world that is religiously very different from the one that first defined his role. His job was conceived in an age of faith, at a time when the United States was largely Christian and understood its mission in religious terms. Chaplains were charged with making sure that fighting men were pious and conducted themselves so as to assure God's blessing on their efforts at war. A chaplain served his troops by defining their fight in spiritual terms, calling them to deeper faith, teaching them a valiant warrior code, and tending their souls in moments of distress.

Today, the chaplain's role is defined only in terms of the personal, the spiritual, and the ceremonial. "I want to talk about how to fight like men and women of God," one chaplain stationed in Iraq said, "but I feel like I can only pray at ceremonies, lead chapel services, and counsel soldiers about their problems. Our nation is in a fight for its life, but I can't stand as the priests did in the Bible and speak to the fight. It's like I can only pray 'Now I lay me down to sleep...' prayers, when I want to pray, 'Lord, rise up against Your enemies' prayers."

This "separation of faith and fight," as one chaplain styled it, is due to a number of factors. The first is military policy. In the Army regulations that define a chaplain's role, it is clear that the personal spiritual life of a soldier is in view and not the spirituality of his life as a warrior. The chaplain is charged with meeting the "religious, spiritual, moral, and ethical needs of the Army." Yet the chaplain is also described as a "noncombatant." He is not allowed to carry arms, and it is clear that his job is essentially that of a civilian pastor in uniform. In fact, he is not even supposed to go near the fighting. Many chaplains strain at these restrictions and feel that they keep them from doing their jobs.

During the Coalition's assault on Fallujah in 2004, one bold chaplain accompanied squads of Marines as they went door to door looking for insurgents. Though the chaplain was unarmed, he entered suspect homes with the Marines and constantly urged courage in their task by quoting scriptures and praying aloud. The warriors he tended loved him for putting himself in harm's way and for sharing the dangers they endured. When this story was reported in the newspapers back home, the chaplain was celebrated as a hero. Pastors mentioned his courageous faith in their sermons, and religious talk-show hosts lauded him on the air. Yet this chaplain was disciplined by his superiors for exposing himself to danger and potentially distracting the men he accompanied from their mission. He was "showboating," his commanders said, and failing to do his job. Privately, this chaplain said, "I was doing my job. What they want is religious window dressing and someone to keep the ceremonial circus up and running. I want to be a prophet to my Marines in the crucible of their lives. I'm no good to them if I don't face what they face when they face it."

101

This forced distance from the fighting only compromises chaplains in the eyes of the Millennials they serve. Millennial faith is already distrustful of tradition, authority, and structure. This is primarily because all three of these seem irrelevant to spirituality as the typical Millennial perceives it. For Millennials at war, the fact that their chaplains cannot "cross the wire," cannot know what they know about being under fire, only makes them even less trustworthy.

The story of faith in one company illustrates this. Based at Camp Seitz just outside of Baghdad, the 1544th Transportation Company has endured some of the most ferocious fighting of the war. It is their job to protect some of the most contested roads in Iraq. Their losses have been heavy, but their fighting spirit is undimmed.

The soldiers in the 1544th are young. The commander of Camp Seitz, Lt. Col. Richard Rael, calls them "college kids." But he says it with respect, and it is a fitting description. Most of the soldiers in this company were indeed sitting in college classrooms when their National Guard units were called up. They had only joined the Illinois National Guard to earn money for college, and now they have left their studies, some just months before graduation, and are enduring fierce fighting and the death of friends they once sat with at the campus watering hole.

The 1544th is a unique example of Millennial faith because while their captain, Brandon Tackett, says he stays out of his soldier's spiritual lives, many under his command are deeply religious. There is Jodi Rund, for example. Corporal Rund is blond, fresh faced, and not hard to imagine as a campus head-turner. Not long ago, she was a sociology major at the University of Illinois. She was called up when she had only one semester left and now finds herself in the thick of the Iraq war. And she is a good soldier. One of her colleagues described her as "Osama bin Laden's worst nightmare: a pretty woman who prays to Jesus and fights as well as any man."

Jodi was raised Catholic and found a new interest in faith when she learned she was fighting for her country in the land of ancient Babylon. She yearned to know more about biblical history, and this brought her to websites that fed her spirit. She began to e-mail Christian friends at home about her faith. Soon she met other Christians in her company. There was David Wetherell, for example, another University of Illinois student who was working on a finance degree when he was called up. Wetherell had "fallen away" from his Christian faith when he was first deployed, but the death of his sergeant on the first day he arrived, and his realization that he might die, moved him to "give my life to Jesus." Now, Rund and Wetherell are part of a Christian group within the 1544th that studies books like Rick Warren's *The Purpose-Driven Life*, passes around sermons from ministers back home, and shares prayer lists together. When one of them is hurt, the rest pray for healing. There have been miracles, they say, and none of them could survive without each other, their deepening faith in Jesus Christ, and the strength they find in their Bibles.

Both Rund and Wetherell have nurtured vibrant spiritual lives in the face of war, but all without the aid of chaplains. Asked about the chaplains he knows, Wetherell replied, "Some are great and some stink, but none of them understand what soldiers go through in the field." Rund reports that chaplains may have their place, but since they aren't involved in the crux of battle, they are not really relevant. "Services don't help," she insists. "Conventional, organized religion doesn't meet our needs. I find that e-mails keep me strong, and the psalms I put on my walls. Some of us get together before going out and pray. This is what keeps me going spiritually. Praying and surviving is the heart of my faith. But there isn't a chaplain around at those times."

Another member of the 1544th, Sergeant John Lauher, is even more pointed when it comes to chaplains. "Most military chaplains talk about the Army and the good that the Army is doing. Who cares? Because they don't have big audiences at memorials, rather than pray and honor the dead, they just turn it into a sermon. They should understand that we've lost a comrade and want to honor him, but because they don't go out with us, they don't understand how we feel. When they turn our memorial into a pep rally, it turns my stomach."

Chaplains, then, are hindered by the policies that keep them from experiencing the stresses of soldiers and by the distrust of authority and structure inherent in Millennial faith. They are also hindered by their own doubts about their roles, and this is often due to the shifting tides of respect for religion in American culture.

One chaplain, who asked not to be identified, explained that this uncertainty among the chaplains' corps often arises because of the military's response to legal pressures:

> Most of us want to talk about the things soldiers need to discuss: Is this war just? Is God on our side? Is killing in this war moral? Are there spiritual forces affecting performance on the battlefield? Is Islam evil? What is right and wrong in the fighting? Yet every time one of these legal cases comes along, there is a chill from the top down, and everyone gets scared that if we do anything more than pray at ceremonies and hold chapel services, we will end up in trouble. It's frustrating. I want to serve fighting men and women while they fight. I don't want to make the sign of the cross from a safe distance. Something's got to change.

105

The legal cases this chaplain alludes to have indeed moved many to reconsider the chaplain's role. The simple problem is that the military chaplaincy is caught in a time warp between modern forces of secularism and the faith of the founding era. Though it is clear that early Americans were largely Christian and wanted faith at the core of society, later generations have moved away from that founding faith and have begun to interpret the Constitution accordingly. In 1971, for example, the U.S. Supreme Court ruled in *Lemon v. Kurtzman*, 403 U.S. 602 (1971), that there are three conditions the government must meet in order not to violate the Establishment Clause of the First Amendment, which prohibits an enforcement of religion by the state. The government's action must: "(1) reflect a clearly secular purpose; (2) have a primary effect that neither advances nor inhibits religion; and (3) avoid excessive government entanglement with religion." Obviously, the military chaplaincy violates each one of these requirements.

This was a point not lost on two Harvard University law students in 1979. Building on the reasoning of *Lemon v. Kurtzman*, Joel Katcoff and Allen Wieder—moved, some said, by a desire to impress their Constitutional law professor—filed a lawsuit designed to challenge the constitutionality of the military chaplaincy. The suit claimed that state-financed chaplains are an establishment of religion and in violation of the First Amendment.

It almost worked. The case dragged on until January of 1986 and was finally dropped only when Katcoff and Wieder ran out of money to fund an appeal. In *Katcoff v. Marsh*, 755 F.2d 223 (2d Cir. 1985), the court ruled that the military chaplaincy should remain in place to fulfill the constitutional guarantee that soldiers have freedom to exercise their religion. The case raised serious fears, though. If two law students who might be merely showing off could nearly eradicate the military chaplaincy, the constitutional basis for the chaplains' corps must be tenuous indeed. Moreover, the majority opinion in the case admitted that the chaplaincy was inconsistent with the three requirements in *Lemon v. Kurtzman*. How long would it be before judges in another case found the chaplaincy in violation of the law?

These matters loom large for military chaplains today. What they are deployed to do is under constant legal scrutiny. In 1972, a small number of cadets and midshipmen from the nation's military academies joined together for a class action suit intended to ban compulsory chapel attendance. The effort was successful, and the resulting case, *Anderson v. Laird*, 466 F.2d 283 (D.C. Cir. 1972), has stood as a warning in the minds of many chaplains that the connection between religious faith and the military may one day be severed. These same fears were awakened in 2001 when the Virginia chapter of the American Civil Liberties Union sued the Virginia Military Institute on behalf of two former cadets who opposed a mandatory prayer before meals. The ACLU won the suit and immediately sent a letter warning the United States Naval Academy that it also must change its tradition of a mandatory prayer before lunch.

These efforts by the ACLU have moved several congressmen to propose a bill designed to protect prayer at the nation's military academies. Representative Walter Jones of North Carolina and Senator Sam Brownback of Kansas have determined that the connection between faith and the training of warriors must not be severed. "I find it incredibly ironic that liberal organizations like the ACLU are attempting to take away the very freedoms that these students are willing to go to war to protect," Rep. Jones said. "The principles of faith that guided our founders animate the lives of the men and women training to defend our nation. That tradition and heritage is in trouble."[21]

Legal cases such as these leave many chaplains with the sense that they are living on borrowed time. "You have the ACLU and the military academy cases on the one hand," a chaplain, who did not want to be named, complained, "and you have the fascination with faith that is thriving in American culture, particularly among the young, on the other hand. Chaplains are in the middle. What do you think they are going to do? They are going to do their job, but sometimes we aren't sure where the First Amendment line is. This makes many of us hesitate to do the job we want to do: speak like prophets to men and women of God in a fight."

This issue of legal definition and the requirement that chaplains stay removed from the fighting have a profound effect on soldiers in the field. As a private in the 1544th Transportation Company at Camp Seitz recounted, "I was having a crisis about what I was doing. I went to a chaplain and asked if he thought God was on our side and if we were really fighting evil by fighting the insurgents. You could see he wasn't sure, or at least that he didn't want to say. He hesitated. Then he said, 'Well, the president says we are fighting for democracy and the values of freedom. So we must be doing a good thing.' I thought to myself, *Man, that's the answer I expected from my government professor back home, not from a spokesman for God.*"

109

Even in war moral power is

to physical as three parts out

of four.

—NAPOLEON BONAPARTE
(1769–1821)

CHAPTER 4

ANVIL OF THE
WARRIOR CODE

I t was 1917 and America had just entered

the First World War. Throughout the nation,

soldiers were preparing for the voyage that

would allow them to defend their nation's

honor across the seas in places like Belgium,

Austria, and France. Knowing that many of these American warriors would never return, and that all of them would need a guide for their conduct in battle, the New York Bible Society determined to give each soldier a pocket New Testament. They also asked former President Theodore Roosevelt, himself an outspoken Christian, to compose a message for the inside cover. His words framed a warrior code for that generation and have come to be known as the *Micah Mandate*.

> The teaching of the New Testament is foreshadowed in Micah's verse, "He has shown you, O man, what is good and what the Lord requires of you: but to do justice and to love mercy, and walk humbly with your God" (Micah 6:8).
>
> Do justice; and therefore fight valiantly against those who stand for the reign of Molech and Beelzebub on this earth.
>
> Love mercy; treat your enemies well, suffer the afflicted, treat every woman as though she were your sister, care for the little children, rescue the perishing, and be tender with the old and helpless.

Walk humbly; you will do so if you study the life and teaching of the Savior, walking in His steps.

Remember, the most perfect machinery of government will not keep us as a nation if there is not within us a soul, no abounding of material prosperity shall avail us if our spiritual sense is atrophied. The foes of our own household will surely prevail against us unless there be in our people an inner life which finds its outward expression in a morality like unto that preached by the seers and the prophets of God when the grandeur that was Greece and the glory that was Rome still lay in the future.[1]

113

In these words, Roosevelt both put the war in spiritual perspective and told America's soldiers what it meant to conduct themselves with honor. He first assured them that they were fighting a system of evil, one demonically empowered like the pagan empires of old. Then he gave them an ethical code, telling them how to treat women, their enemies, the weak, and the dying. And he called them to live humbly, to realize that success in battle, much like success in life, depends upon honoring the God who rules men's destinies.

This concise charge became a creed and a warrior code for men in the field. They quoted it to each other in times of duress and took their New Testaments home to give them to the children they would one day have. The words captured the dream of a civilization distilled into the kind of code a warrior can live.

Eighty-eight years later, a battle-weary sergeant in Iraq was shown Roosevelt's words on a reporter's Palm Pilot. "God," he said, the admiration obvious in his voice, "I wish we had such a thing for our war."

Lt. Col. Robert Patterson was relieved. It was finally over. For two years he had served as President Bill Clinton's Air Force aide, but now it was time to go. It was supposed to be an enviable assignment, this opportunity to work at the president's side and carry the "football"—the briefcase-sized device from which a president can order a nuclear strike. The job was an honor, proof of the nation's trust. But Patterson was glad to be leaving. He simply could not stand to see the military dishonored any more.

Yet, as Patterson has relayed in his best-selling book *Dereliction of Duty*, low regard for the armed forces was sometimes present in the Clinton administration. For example, the Clintons had seriously considered banning all military uniforms from the White House. Even the Marines who had guarded the president's home for decades were slated for reassignment. Then someone observed that the American people might not like it, and the idea was laid aside. There was also the time when pilots were left waiting on overseas runways for the authority to launch a secret mission. But permission never came. Why? It was reported that the president was watching a golf tournament. High-ranking officers were often sent scurrying on menial errands, and during one period no one could find the launch codes that enabled the president to defend the nation in case of nuclear attack. Clinton had misplaced them.[2]

115

No, Patterson was glad to be going. He had seen enough. The Air Force, knowing what he had endured, decided to offer him a plum assignment as a squadron commander. He had something different in mind, though, and asked his superiors to assign him to the United States Air Force Academy.

"I wanted to go back to the roots," Patterson explained, "back to the origins of officership, integrity, and honor. It was important to me to reclaim my pride, my self-respect, and I decided the best way to accomplish that would be by teaching future officer candidates the meaning of honor, integrity, and character. I wanted to return to the naïveté and innocence of college-aged men and women just starting out in their pursuit of the profession of arms. I wanted to wake up each morning and, as General Fogleman so aptly put it when he retired, ask myself, *Do I feel honorable and clean?* and be able to answer yes."[3]

What Patterson yearned for and hoped to find again at the Air Force Academy was what draws many men and women to a military life. It is the completion that comes from living by a code, from aligning one's life with a set of principles that elevate and ennoble and make that life of impact. It is devotion to the path of an exceptional life.

 The warrior code takes a soldier and makes him a knight. It connects the natural life of a fighter to a supernatural understanding of the warrior calling. His duties are transformed into holy sacrifices; his sense of self is reformed into an image of the servant in pursuit of valor. He becomes part of a fellowship, a noble tradition that flows through him and carries him beyond the mediocre and the vain.

This living by a code is an intoxicating experience. In a tent at Camp Anaconda in Iraq, a young soldier sits quietly on his bunk contemplating the few hours he has left before rotating home. His tour of duty is done; his days in the Army at an end. But tears begin to form in his eyes, and when one of his comrades asks what is wrong, he says, "I am afraid that I will never be this alive again, that I will never know this kind of purpose when I get up in the morning. Is my whole life going to be common from now on?"

What this soldier has tasted is a level of nobility and honor his civilian life at home does not offer. He has been part of the profession at arms. He feels himself connected to the greatness of his country, to his president, to men and women who have given their lives, to a value system that takes every duty, no matter how mundane, and elevates it to an offering. He has guidelines, principles, procedures, and standards that define his life. He's not sure he will ever have them again.

117

When the American armed forces conduct themselves by this code, they are an inspiration to the American people. This is the military small towns celebrate in parades and presidents laud in Memorial Day speeches. It is why visitors stream to America's battlefields each year and teenagers stand by their grandparents at monuments and press their fingers into the inscriptions. When airport crowds applaud khaki-clad soldiers home from Afghanistan and students in elementary school classrooms write letters to men and women in the field, this is the image they have in their minds: an army of patriots putting themselves in harm's way for the nation they love and all in the service of their God.

When the armed forces live beneath their code, the American people can become angry. And Hollywood often captures their rage. In films like *Taps*, *Platoon*, *Apocalypse Now*, and *Born on the Fourth of July*, this hope for nobility but rage at dishonor is portrayed. The film *A Few Good Men* is a case in point.

In this movie, Jack Nicholson portrays a decorated Marine colonel who is under investigation because a private has died in his command. While testifying in court, Nicholson's character reacts angrily to an attorney, played by Tom Cruise, who suspects that the private died because of the colonel's orders. The issue quickly becomes a matter of who has honor. The colonel contends, "We use words like honor, code, loyalty...we use these words as the backbone to a life spent defending something. You use 'em as a punch line."[4] The colonel is right about this code, and Americans watching the film yearn for a military that lives by this code. It turns out, though, that the colonel is hiding behind the words. He is guilty and has hoped to throw Cruise's character off track by posturing.

A more pointed example of this same hypocrisy comes earlier in the film. The dead private's lieutenant, played by Kiefer Sutherland, explains why the man is dead: "Commander, I believe in God, and in His Son Jesus Christ, and because I do, I can say this: Private

Santiago is dead, and that's a tragedy. But he's dead because he had no code. He's dead because he had no honor. And God was watching."[5] These words are a reflection of the values Americans hope their soldiers believe, but in the film they are a lie. The lieutenant too is guilty and is hiding behind a smoke screen of honor.

What most Americans yearn for is an armed force of men and women who live by a code of honor, one that takes ethical boundaries, inspiration to excellence, love of country, a sense of heritage, and reverence for God and combines them into a noble martial lifestyle. Clearly, the new warriors in the field yearn for the same thing. Perhaps this is why one of the streets at Camp Victory in Iraq is named William Wallace Boulevard. The Millennials, having acquired their ideals from movies more than any other generation, are inspired by the legend of *Braveheart* and want to connect their efforts in Iraq to this valiant figure. This may also be why the film *The Last Samurai* is a favorite among soldiers in Iraq and Afghanistan today. This film lauds the Bushido code of Shintoism, a warrior code that appeals to Millennials in desperate search of a connection between invisible truth and their lives as professional fighters.

In fact, if the modern military does not offer its warriors a more spiritual code, it can expect the new generation at war to reach for the codes of nontraditional faiths to fill the void. This is because what passes for a warrior code in the modern military fails them. To be of any value to the Millennials, their code must be practical but also inspirational. It must connect to the spiritual sense their generation cherishes, but it must certainly avoid preachy, airy phrases that have no vital meaning. It must also have a sense of history. It is the Millennials, teamed with their boomer parents, who have fed an American fascination with history evidenced by film, monuments, literature, and political debate, after all. Finally, their code must be ethical, giving them a moral compass, a systematized wisdom to compensate for the relative aimlessness of their times.

What the military currently offers is far beneath the comprehensive code the Millennials need to integrate faith, ethics, and military lore into a meaningful system. The Army, for example, emphasizes both a seven-point list of "Army Values" and a "Soldier's Creed." The seven "Values" are:[6]

> **LOYALTY**: Bear truth, faith, and allegiance to the U.S. Constitution, the Army, your unit, and other Soldiers.

> **DUTY**: Fulfill your obligations.

> **RESPECT**: Treat people as they should be treated.

SELFLESS SERVICE: Put the welfare of the nation, the Army, and your subordinates before your own.

HONOR: Live up to all the Army Values.

INTEGRITY: Do what's right, legally and morally.

PERSONAL COURAGE: Face fear, danger, or adversity (physical or moral).

As a Christian chaplain in Iraq said, "The problem with the seven Army Values is that they are a list of dos and don'ts. If a soldier is a person of faith already, he or she can integrate this list of ethics into his broader faith and have something workable. If he or she isn't devoted to a faith, then this list is no different from any other Army regulation. The only difference is that the list asks for moral conduct and sacrifice that isn't usually possible for human beings without some higher truth in their lives."

Perhaps because some in the upper ranks of the Army recognize that what this chaplain has said is true, soldiers are also given a "Soldier's Creed."[7]

I am an American soldier.

I am a Warrior and a member of a
team.

I serve the people of the United States
   and live the Army Values.
I will always place the mission first.
I will never accept defeat.
I will never quit.
I will never leave a fallen comrade.
I am disciplined, physically and men-
   tally tough, trained and proficient
   in my warrior tasks and drills.
I always maintain my arms, my equip-
   ment, and myself.
I am an expert and I am a professional.
I stand ready to deploy, engage, and
   destroy the enemies of the United
   States of America in close combat.
I am a guardian of freedom and the
   American way of life.
I am an American soldier.

122

These Values and this Creed are printed on pieces of metal shaped like dog tags and on cards that soldiers keep in their wallets. They are intended to inspire and align the vision of America's fighters. Yet there is no mention of faith, no mention of the morality of killing in certain circumstances, no mention of a spiritual understanding of the profession of arms, and no calling to righteous conduct toward the dying, the weak, civilians, or a captured enemy. Yet chaplains know that these are the critical issues that soldiers deal with in the field and that distinguish confident fighters from the hesitant and the uncertain.

Both the Values and the Creed are similar to a coach's inspirational charge before a sporting event. What soldiers need, though, is an ennobling of their profession through the integration of faith and the moral vision that faith provides. Soldiers can be trained to do their jobs by repetition and drill. The moral vision for that job, though, comes through a commitment to the profession of arms that is rooted in religious ideals. As George Washington said in his famous Farewell Address: "Let us with caution indulge the supposition that morality can be maintained without religion."[8]

123

It is precisely because the military's light version of a warrior code falls short of what modern warriors need that the words of General William Boykin have resonated so loudly in today's armed forces. Though he certainly did not intend to do so, Gen. Boykin gave many in the field just the kind of warrior code they needed to fulfill their duties with moral passion. The fact that this single Christian voice has had such a profound effect and stirred such wide controversy is testament to the lack of a faith-based warrior code in this generation.

In 2003, Gen. Boykin accepted invitations from churches throughout the United States to speak about the state of the conflicts in Afghanistan and Iraq. He later said that he accepted these invitations because he thought he could ease the concerns of the parents of America's soldiers and because he wanted to offer perspective that Americans were not getting in the mainstream media. Boykin thought he would be speaking to the congregations of Christian churches only, and his comments were designed to appeal to that audience alone. Video recordings of his speeches quickly reached major television networks, though, and soon the general's comments were being reported on CBS's flagship news program, *60 Minutes*, and debated on the floor of Congress.

Boykin's comments received wide attention not only for their incendiary nature but also because he is a soldier's soldier, a man dearly loved in America's elite military forces like the SEALS, the Rangers, and the Delta Force. The general was there when an attempt to rescue Americans held hostage in Iran, called "Desert One," failed miserably, and he was the commander of the elite Delta Force during the horrendous firefight in Mogadishu that claimed world attention in 1993. By the time Boykin began speaking in churches in

2003, he was a highly decorated three-star general, the undersecretary of defense for intelligence, and a beloved inspiration to American warriors around the world.

In each of his speeches, Boykin began by describing his own soldier's story. He recounted that he heard God call him into the Delta Force when he was a young captain. "There are times when God speaks to you in an audible voice," Boykin explained. "He spoke to me that morning because I said, 'Satan is gathering his forces.' He [God] said, 'Yes, son, but so am I.' And I knew I was to be there." The general went on to speak of the importance of prayer in his work. "I wake up every morning about 4:30 a.m., and I pray for about a half an hour, and I pray again before I go to bed at night. And during the day, I take opportunities to pray also."

Boykin believes his discipline in prayer has meant the difference between life and death on some occasions. During the heaviest of the fighting in Mogadishu, Boykin survived a mortar explosion that immediately killed one of his men and left another bleeding to death. "There was no pulse. There was no pressure. But I prayed to Almighty God [to] spare him," said Boykin in his speech. "Today, he practices medicine in the Shenandoah Valley and has four children."

Boykin also told about an earlier time, during the disaster of Desert One, in which he again believes

125

prayer made the difference. In the attempt to rescue the American hostages in Iran, a helicopter collided with a transport plane filled with soldiers. "It was a huge ball of fire. They could not survive," recalls Boykin. "That aircraft was going to explode any moment. But as I prayed in the name of Jesus, the door of that aircraft opened and through those flames came forty-five men running just as hard as they could."

It was as Boykin told some of these stories from his past that he began to articulate his worldview. He described chasing a warlord during the 1993 fighting in Somalia. "I knew my God was bigger than his. I knew that my God was a real God and his was an idol." Though Boykin later explained that the "idol" in this warlord's life was not Allah, the Muslim God, but rather money and greed, the general's comments nevertheless expressed a belief in war as a contest of spiritual forces.

The general continued to articulate his spiritual understanding of history and war in explaining the hatred that greets Americans in much of the world. "Why do they hate us so much? I will tell you this. This is my own personal belief. One of the most fundamental reasons they hate us is (a) because we are a nation of believers, and (b) because we support Israel. Now, if you don't believe that this nation was founded on Christian beliefs, Christian values, then go back and read the writings and the orations of the founders of this nation; read what they said. Every man that signed the Constitution of the United States was of the Christian faith."

Having established a Christian vision of the nation's history, Boykin then explained the presidency of George W. Bush in distinctly biblical terms. "You must recognize that we as Americans saw a miracle unfold with the election of George W. Bush. Whether you voted for him or not is irrelevant. The fact is he is there today not only to lead America, but to lead the world, and that is what he is doing. Where does he start his day? He starts his day in the Oval Office at 4:30 with a Bible in his hand."

Finally, Boykin expressed his view that America's military conflicts abroad are spiritual as well as physical. Showing a PowerPoint slide of Osama bin Laden to his church audience, Boykin said, "We as Americans, we as Christians, need to understand that that's not the enemy that America's up against. We are in fact in a spiritual battle, ladies and gentlemen, more than we are in a physical battle."

When comments such as these reached the public, Boykin was called an embarrassment, a three-star bigot, and a born-again bumpkin. Senator John Warner, a Republican from Virginia, and Senator Richard Durbin of Illinois suggested that the general should be reassigned. An internal Pentagon investigation concluded that Boykin's comments should have been cleared in advance, and the Secretary of the Army issued a "letter of concern." Even President Bush found it necessary to issue a statement assuring that General Boykin "doesn't reflect my point of view or the point of view of this administration."

During the height of the controversy over his words, Boykin gave few interviews but did appear on *60 Minutes* to explain his intentions. Then he receded from view. The media, and the American people's interest, turned to other matters. What went unnoticed was the attention Boykin's words received among those fighting in Afghanistan and Iraq.

What Boykin had unintentionally accomplished was the fashioning of a warrior code, or at least the closest thing to a faith-based code as has been presented to the new generation at war. He first offered himself as a model of the Christian officer, a man of prayer, piety, miracles, and a distinctly Christian vision for his profession. Then he articulated the nation in spiritual terms. "America is a Christian nation," he said, "with a calling under the hand of God. Her battles, then, are spiritual and should be fought by men and women who comprise a 'Christian army.'"

Many soldiers in the field got the message. They were desperate for spiritual leadership and desperate for models of the moral man of war. Boykin fit the bill. His sermons, as vilified as they were in the American press, were quietly absorbed by soldiers in the field as the spiritual vision they needed for their fight. As one lieutenant colonel serving at USCENTCOM at Mac-Dill Air Force Base in Florida said, "I won't say it publicly, and you can't use my name, but I will tell you that I agree with everything Boykin said. In fact, I don't know many here who wouldn't. Most of us would give anything if the chaplains or our commanders would speak to us in the same terms Boykin did. What he gave us was the spiritual map we needed."

A chaplain with the 3rd Corps in Iraq said, "I don't think Jerry was wise in going public with his comments, but I'll tell you that what he said was true. You'd find most soldiers here aligning with some version of Boykin's worldview."

While Boykin's comments were powerfully delivered, the tragedy is that he alone should be the voice offering young soldiers a model, a "spiritual map," for their thinking about war and the conduct of warriors. Clearly, there is a void into which an officially secular military may not speak, into which chaplains are prevented from speaking, and in which either informal Millennial faiths or strong personalities like Boykin take command. However the policy makers for the

American military may view Boykin and his comments, the fact is that soldiers in the field resonated with him because they have been offered little else. In an age of Millennial spirituality, in an age of nontraditional religions increasing in strength, and in an age when America is facing a religiously charged enemy, this is a dangerous condition.

What, then, should provide the basis of a faith-based warrior code? If the modern military should hear General Boykin's wake-up call and fashion a religiously informed code of its own, where should the process begin?

Clearly, the foundation of any religiously influenced warrior code is a theology of war. A nation must determine the moral basis for waging war if it is to ask its warriors to conduct themselves morally. The moral basis for war and moral conduct in the war are connected. The one draws from the other. Any nation that wages war without moral consideration, but demands moral conduct from its warriors, asks the impossible. It would be more consistent to simply discard morality in the conduct of war and return to the amorality of barbarian warrior cultures.

Fortunately, there have been centuries of study and reflection on this matter of a theology of war. Starting with Augustine in the fourth century and continuing with Thomas Aquinas in the thirteenth century, the Christian church has evolved a theology of war known as the *Just War Theory*. Augustine first formulated this theory in his classic *The City of God*, in which he suggested that there are two questions that a moral people must ask about war. First, "When is it permissible to wage war, *jus in bello*?" and, second, "What are the limitations on the ways we wage war, *jus ad bellum*?" The answers to these two questions provide the basis of any warrior code.

For Augustine, the first requirement for a just war was proper authority. As he put it: "The natural order, which is suited to the peace of moral things, requires that the authority and deliberation for undertaking war be under the control of a leader."[9] The leader Augustine had in mind was one whom God had entrusted with the responsibility of governance. In his time, this was the emperor. Later, it would be kings and princes. Today, it would be elected officials.

Second, for Augustine, there had to be a proper cause for war. He specifically ruled out as justifications for war such causes as "the desire for harming, the cruelty of revenge, the restless and implacable mind, the savageness of revolting, and the lust for dominating." Augustine saw war as a tragic necessity, and so he admonished rulers to "let necessity slay the warring foe, not your will."[10]

Third, Augustine required that there be a reasonable chance of success. Even with good reason to attack, a nation cannot simply send young men to die, he argued. Human life is too precious, too sacred to waste. Augustine's final requirement was one of proportionality. In waging a war, he argued that authorities must make sure that the harm caused by their response to aggression does not exceed the harm caused by the aggression itself.

A warrior code of any moral depth must be built on a theology of war at least similar to that of Augustine. Warriors must have the confidence that their rulers will not wage war without just reason. To do otherwise makes the soldier a mercenary and dissolves any moral resolve, any intention to apply principles of honor to the conduct in war. The war becomes about dominance and the will to power, and this motivation filters down into the daily conduct of soldiers in the field. How civilians, the wounded, the dying, and the captured enemy are treated becomes an extension of the immorality that informed the waging of the war in the first place. Barbarity reigns. Slaughter and rape become commonplace. This is exactly what the Just War theory intended to prevent.

When the Bush administration began making its case for the invasion of Iraq, there was some consideration of the Just War theory. Jim Nicholson, the U.S. ambassador to the Holy See in Rome, invited economist and Catholic lay-theologian Michael Novak to give a lecture in a series sponsored by the embassy on the evening of February 10, 2003. His subject was the Christian Just War doctrine with specific reference to Iraq. Novak's speech was a brilliant exposition of the Augustinian theory of war as it has been applied through the ages, the contemporary applicability of those teachings, and the moral moorings of the Bush Doctrine.

Oddly, this approach was not taken in justifying the war to the American people or to the soldiers who were about to be deployed. Instead, the case to the American public was made on the basis of the Bush Doctrine— "Those who support the terrorists will share their fate"— the need for freedom in the world, and the presence of weapons of mass destruction. This choice to sidestep the Just War theory in justifying the invasion of Iraq was a surprising decision given that President Bush is an evangelical Christian and that his administration is more "faith-based" than any in recent history.

Augustine's second question—"What are the limitations on the ways we wage war, *jus ad bellum*?"—is the second pillar in the construction of a warrior code. Once a moral war is declared, how should soldiers conduct themselves accordingly? Augustine maintained that the just conduct of war required two primary values: discrimination and proportionality. This question of discrimination concerns the decision as to who are legitimate targets in war. In a moral war, there must be a decision as to who may legitimately be killed. War is about the killing of combatants. However, there are noncombatants, civilians, the wounded, the captured, and the elderly who may not be killed if moral considerations are any guide.

A second matter in the moral limiting of warrior conduct is that of proportionality. The goal of proportionality is to limit overall suffering, to restrict the damage of combat to combatants. War naturally inflames rage and vengeance. The question of proportionality serves as a moral filter on strategic decisions and keeps baser human emotions from carrying the horrors of war outside of proper boundaries.

These two Augustinian questions regarding war are essential to a warrior code because they provide the moral framework for the lives of soldiers. Guided by these values, the military may then evolve a profession of arms that is intended to create "righteous warriors" of sufficient skill, character, and devotion to execute war justly and effectively. This profession must connect the duties of soldiers to the spiritual vision of knights in a righteous cause. Accordingly, soldiers discipline their bodies to the glory of God and to kill their nation's enemies effectively. They learn to shoot well to dispatch enemies but also to limit unnecessary killing, an extension of the moral justification for war. They obey authority because they view that authority as ordained by God and as a force for good in their lives and the life of their nation. They conduct themselves bravely in war because they believe themselves in service of a righteous cause, as warriors with a purpose greater than national pride or economic gain.

This profession of arms and the warrior code that defines it must also have a sense of continuity, of connection to fighting men and women of the past. A chaplain in the field serves more sacrificially and passionately for knowing the story of the *Dorchester's* "immortal four." A Ranger goes into battle ennobled by the life and devotion of Captain Russell Rippetoe. A sergeant at Camp Seitz in Iraq is buoyed by what he knows of minutemen in the American Revolution or of the courage of POWs in Vietnam. The history of men and women in arms grants an impartation to his life, frames his sense of professionalism, and moves him to serve a dream greater than any one presidential administration or war as he puts himself willingly in danger.

This sense of faith-inspired professionalism, rooted in history and elevated by a holy vision, is burned into the individual soul and into the heart of the culture through rituals. Like the vigil of the medieval knight of old, there must be the rituals that welcome men and women to arms, celebrate their victories, honor their sacrifices, and extend their memory. A holy warrior code must literally be fashioned on the altar of worship. It must be shaped on the anvil of a discipline held before a watching God. This is as true for the warrior as it is for the nation as a whole.

This latter point is played out every day at the Tomb of the Unknown Soldier at Arlington National Cemetery in Washington DC. During the Changing of the Guard Ceremony, visitors are asked to stand at attention and in silence to honor their nation's dead. If a photographer kneels or someone speaks during the ceremony, the sergeant in charge rebukes the crowd and calls them to attention. The lesson is clear: "Respect for those who fight and die is expected of all citizens. Stand in silence, and remember the price of your freedom."

Finally, once a nation has committed itself to morality in war and to a profession of arms that is both holy and powerful, it must then feed this warrior culture with an inspiring poetic expression. If Disraeli was right that "men govern by words," then it must also be true that men fight for words, as well. Words describe purpose and values for a warrior. This is why a muddy corporal in Northern Iraq explained himself by quoting a line from one of his president's speeches. "The commitment of our fathers is now the calling of our time,"[11] he said, when asked why he fought. It is also why a medic at Camp Anaconda tearfully explained her role by citing the day shortly after the horrors of September 11, 2001, when George W. Bush told workers at Ground Zero that the "whole world" would hear them soon. "I'm part of what the world is hearing," this medic insisted. "I'm part of the American voice in this part of the world. I wouldn't want to be anywhere else."

The truth is that warriors must struggle constantly to remain inspired. They face such hardships, such drudgery interrupted by tragedy, that they must have fuel to stoke their inner fires. Words are that fuel. From presidential speeches to the sermons of ministers, from snippets of poetry to slogans from warriors past, soldiers cling to the words that frame their experience with meaning and move them to heroism in the field.

Certainly the master of inspiring a nation and an army with words was Winston Churchill. An example of his power—his "artillery of words," as one author termed it—was recounted by a soldier who attended Winston Churchill's funeral in 1965.

> I was a subaltern at Dunkirk and the Nazis kicked my unit to death. We left everything behind when we got out; some of my men didn't even have boots. They dumped us along the roads near Dover, and all of us were scared and dazed, and the memory of the Panzers could set us screaming at night. Then he [Churchill] got on the radio and said we'd fight on the beaches and in the towns and that we'd never surrender. And I cried when I heard him. I'm not ashamed to say it. And I thought, to hell with the Panzers— we're going to win![12]

138

This is what a nation's leaders must do to feed the noble warriors it sends into battle: inspire them with the poetic words that capture the meaning of their fight. In fact, when the words of leaders grow dull and bureaucratic, soldiers usually answer their need for inspiration themselves by developing an oral tradition of poetry and song. The tale of one famous speech portrays this well.

The famous Agincourt Speech of Shakespeare's *Henry V* has become one of the most influential examples of martial poetry and verse in modern history. Shakespeare fashioned the speech from memoirs and histories of the famous battle of Agincourt of 1415 in which

English troops faced and defeated an overwhelmingly superior French army. In the play, Shakespeare's King Henry gives a speech before the battle that has come to be known as the "St. Crispin's Day Speech."

> That he which hath no stomach to
>   this fight,
> Let him depart; his passport shall be
>   made
> And crowns for convoy put into his purse:
> We would not die in that man's company
> That fears his fellowship to die with us.
> This day is called the feast of Crispian:
> He that outlives this day, and comes safe
>   home,
> Will stand a tip-toe when the day is
>   named,
> And rouse him at the name of Crispian.
> He that shall live this day, and see old
>   age,
> Will yearly on the vigil feast his neigh-
>   bours,
> And say 'To-morrow is Saint Crispian:'
> Then will he strip his sleeve and show
>   his scars.
> And say 'These wounds I had on
>   Crispin's day.'

139

Old men forget: yet all shall be forgot,
But he'll remember with advantages
What feats he did that day: then shall
    our names.
Familiar in his mouth as household
    words
Harry the king, Bedford and Exeter,
Warwick and Talbot, Salisbury and
    Gloucester,
Be in their flowing cups freshly
    remember'd.
This story shall the good man teach
    his son;
And Crispin Crispian shall ne'er go by,
From this day to the ending of the
    world,
But we in it shall be remember'd;
We few, we happy few, we band of
    brothers;
For he to-day that sheds his blood with
    me
Shall be my brother; be he ne'er so vile,
This day shall gentle his condition:
And gentlemen in England now a-bed
Shall think themselves accursed they
    were not here,

And hold their manhoods cheap whiles
    any speaks
That fought with us upon Saint
    Crispin's day.

The St. Crispin's Day Speech has become one of the most influential pieces of martial verse in Western history. Its call to valor, its insistence on viewing the sacrifices of the day in the light of years, and its lauding of the "band of brothers" in war have all resonated with warriors through the centuries. On June 6, 1944, a British officer read the speech to his men just before they stormed the beaches of Normandy and faced murderous machine gun fire. Almost fifty years later, Major General William F. Garrison recited the speech at a memorial service for eighteen American soldiers killed in a violent shootout on the streets of Mogadishu, Somalia.

In Iraq, a captain who majored in literature and drama in college movingly recites the speech each time his company goes into combat. His soldiers have come to love it, and they eagerly call for it once the order to "move out" is given. They too find its call to valor an inspiration. They too celebrate its love of the band of brothers. And they too hope to remember their scars years hence, as these words nearly five hundred years old urge them to do.

The larger point is that a warrior code is inspired by poetry and verse, by the words of leaders, by the verbal art of a people who have come to understand the glory of the warrior calling. They must, in the terms John F. Kennedy once used of Churchill, mobilize the English language and send it into battle.

These four elements of a warrior code—the commitment to wage only just wars, the commitment to justice in the conduct of war, the creation of a holy and historic profession of arms, and the art of serving that profession with an artillery of words—are desperately needed by the Millennial generation serving America overseas today. They are, as we have seen, as patriotic, as informed, and as eager to serve as any generation the nation has produced. But they have been given no code, no moral or spiritual framing for the profession they now find themselves in or the war they now face death to win. They deserve better. Without a warrior code that is mystical, ethical, historic, and social, they will fashion individual codes of their own from the informal religions they already hold. Neither they nor the nation will be well served by this. The danger will not be an absence of code. It will be a code fashioned by vengeance and rage in the heat of battle, and it will only produce more My Lai massacres and more Abu Ghraib prison scandals, as we shall now see.

Morality is contraband in war.

—Mohandas K. Gandhi (1869–1948)

CHAPTER 5

BREAKING CODE

Joe Darby was horrified. The pictures he discovered on a friend's computer sickened him. But he knew what to do. As his family later said, "Joe is a good boy. He knows right from wrong." So Joe did the right thing, and he gave the pictures to the proper authorities.

He could not have known, though, the firestorm his actions would incite. For Joe is Specialist Joe Darby of the 800th Military Police Brigade, and what he had discovered on a fellow soldier's computer were pictures of prisoners being abused and tortured at Abu Ghraib prison in Iraq.

When these pictures became public in April of 2004, the world was as sickened as Joe Darby had been. The photos were undeniable evidence that something had gone terribly wrong. Prisoners were stacked naked like so much firewood and placed in mock positions of torture. One female soldier was pictured brazenly pointing her fingers like a gun at a naked prisoner's genitals. Another picture showed prisoners who were staged so that it appeared they were engaging in oral sex. Other cruelties were also depicted, and it did not take long to realize what kind of culture had prevailed at Abu Ghraib.

Accusations soon filled the airwaves. Some said the behavior of the guards at Abu Ghraib were the moral extensions of the Bush administration's foolish invasion of Iraq. Others said the scandal was evidence of how this new generation of soldiers was immoral and untrustworthy. The previous Clinton administration took a beating, as did Congress, the Pentagon, and even the press for reporting the story in the first place. Blame was easy to find. Answers were far scarcer.

In a tent at Camp Bucca some one hundred fifty miles away, a group of soldiers saw the Abu Ghraib pictures for the first time. The grief that filled their souls was painfully etched into each face. "I suppose now this is how we are going to be remembered," one of them said sadly. "They spit on my father when he came home from Vietnam, and all because of what a few soldiers did at My Lai. Now, no matter what we do here, Abu Ghraib is always going to be stamped over our lives."

147

When the U.S. ambassador to Iraq, Paul Bremer, chose Abu Ghraib as a prison for captured insurgents, he did so because it meant that military vehicles would not have to travel the more contested roads around Baghdad to get there. Situated just twelve miles outside of Baghdad and near Camps Victory and Seitz, Abu Ghraib seemed a perfect facility. Though under Saddam Hussein's regime it had been a place of torture and prolonged imprisonment, this must have made it all the more appealing. Although Abu Ghraib served as the holding pen for thousands of detained Iraqis, many of whom were not former members of Saddam's regime, somehow it seemed poetically just to detain

some insurgents in the very prison meant for their enemies. Yet Ambassador Bremer could not have known
how the legacy of Saddam would haunt the Americans
at Abu Ghraib.

By the time the 800th Military Police Brigade was
assigned to Abu Ghraib, they had received little advance
notice, and few soldiers among them were ready for duty.
As the now famous Schlesinger Panel's report revealed,
the 800th was certified for duty without proper training for their responsibilities at the prison. Even if they
had been, though, they could not have been prepared
for the state of things at Abu Ghraib. The walls in
many of the cells were covered with bloodstains from
Saddam's tortures. Chains still dangled from iron rings
in rooms where suspected spies had been butchered.
Huge pictures of Saddam Hussein, which had been
hung so high that they were difficult to remove, hov-
ered over the larger rooms of the prison, and more than
one American soldier commented that you could feel
Saddam's "evil spirit" moving through the halls.

Conditions at Abu Ghraib fell far short of those
enjoyed by soldiers at nearby camps. The food, by all
accounts, was abysmal, and this was true while, just a
few miles away, soldiers at Camp Victory were enjoying
meals that rivaled those served in some restaurants at
home. What passed for weights in the "fitness center"

were actually tin cans filled with concrete. The lightly attended chapel service took place under a leering picture of Saddam.

Making matters worse was the fact that Abu Ghraib was a prison for suspected insurgents in a hostile zone. This meant that the men and women of the 800th Military Police Brigade not only guarded prisoners but also did so under almost constant threat of attack. In July of 2003 alone, the prison came under mortar attack twenty-five times. On August 16 of that same year, five detainees were killed and sixty-seven were wounded in series of strikes. An attack on April 20, 2004, left some twenty-two detainees dead. Overall, five Americans were killed in bombardments, and the loss of these comrades was never far from the minds of the guards at Abu Ghraib.

As though these strains were not enough, the tragic ratio between guards and detainees created a nearly unmanageable situation. Some ninety personnel had been assigned to Abu Ghraib from the 800th Military Police Brigade. Yet nearly seven thousand prisoners were kept at the facility, meaning that there was, on average, one guard for every seventy-five prisoners. This was far beneath military policy and far from a workable arrangement even in the best of conditions, much less in a war zone.

Adding to the deplorable conditions at Abu Ghraib was a crisis of leadership. As the Schlesinger Panel concluded, "A lax and dysfunctional command climate took hold."[1] By all accounts, senior officers were often hard to find, and the core values of the mission were rarely defined. Soldiers guarding prisoners were left for long periods of time without supervision. Morale was at an unprecedented low for the 800th. Boredom, anger, and disillusionment reigned.

Igniting this powder keg of dysfunction was the pressure the guards felt from military intelligence officers to "break the spirit" of the prisoners. It was well known that among the detainees at Abu Ghraib were men who had killed Americans and served Saddam Hussein in taking innocent lives. This produced a natural animosity among the guards, a quiet rage that exploded into abusive behavior when intelligence officers urged the guards to be "violent and hard."

And so it began. While the night shift was on duty at Cell Block 1, soldiers began stripping detainees, positioning them for lewd photographs, and making them lie on each other naked. Later, when one of the guards was asked why they did such things, he said simply, "Just for the fun of it." There was little supervision and less accountability. So the games continued, night after night, until finally Specialist Joe Darby discovered his friend's pictures and knew he had to make it all stop.

These are the basic facts of the Abu Ghraib prison scandal as they are presented in the Schlesinger Panel's report and as they have surfaced in interviews with guards at the scene. They are not offered to ameliorate guilt. The Abu Ghraib scandal was a violation of everything that the United States and its efforts in Iraq ought to mean. It was a collapse of command, a failure of individual character, and a violation of American values. It may indeed, as the young soldier at Camp Bucca sadly predicted, mark the new generation at war in the eyes of history.

151

Perhaps a greater misfortune, though, would be a refusal to learn the lessons of Abu Ghraib and thus allow such scandals to reoccur. It is too easy to see this tragedy in isolation. To blame only that particular group of soldiers and that particular chain of command, though, misses the point that men and women under dire stress—without moral leadership, without core values held before them, and without a noble sense of mission—may well descend into barbarism. There is too much evidence throughout human history to conclude otherwise.

The famous Stanford Prison Experiment has already proven this case and proven it in unforgettable terms. In 1971, Philip Zimbardo, a professor of psychology at Stanford University, designed an experiment in which twenty-four completely healthy students were assigned roles as either guards or prisoners in an unofficial prison. The study began with the realistic arrest of the prisoner-students by the cooperating Palo Alto Police Department and continued with their internment in a "prison" that had been constructed in the basement of the Psychology Department on the Stanford campus. The prisoners wore standard prison clothing and were assigned numbers for identification. The guards wore military-style uniforms and silver-reflecting sunglasses to enhance anonymity. Both guards and prisoners understood they were merely playing a role.

Zimbardo had designed the study to last two weeks. He stopped it after six days. The results were astonishing. The student-guards began almost immediately treating the student-prisoners with sadistic glee. Prisoners were stripped, hooded, chained, denied food or bedding, put into solitary confinement, and made to clean toilets with their bare hands. Moreover, as boredom set in, guards began to create ever more degrading games with which to torture the prisoners. In time, these amusements turned sexual. Guards forced the prisoners to simulate sodomy on each other and drove them into other deviant forms of behavior.

The experiment revealed striking changes in behavior. Though every participant had been judged psychologically and physically healthy after thorough testing, it was not uncommon for a student who knew he was playing a role as a guard to transform into a sadistic authoritarian. Perfectly normal, "good old boy" prisoners, chosen for their easy-going manner, came close to emotional breakdowns for the treatment they endured. Perhaps most surprising, "good guards," who did not mistreat the prisoners and knew that the abuse was unjust, refused to confront their fellow guards and allowed evil to ripen without challenge.

The parallels between the Stanford Prison Experiment and the Abu Ghraib scandal are obvious. In both situations, there existed a lack of moral restraint enforced by sound leadership and clear values. In both, unsupervised, under-trained guards abused prisoners for entertainment. In both events, this abuse turned sexual. Just as important, in both situations those who judged the treatment of prisoners as wrong did not speak up and in some cases participated in the abuse.

What the story of Abu Ghraib indicates and the memory of the Stanford Prison Experiment confirms is that when human beings are under stress and lack moral reinforcement, horrible things may occur. This is perhaps the strongest case for a faith-based warrior code. War is stress in the extreme. Men and women engaged in war will lean to their baser drives unless they are kept in touch with a more noble vision through moral leadership, a clear set of values, and commitment to an honorable code that guides their lives and their profession.

A largely unknown backstory to the Abu Ghraib prison scandal confirms this need for moral reinforcement under stress. Lieutenant Colonel Daniel W. Taylor, a chaplain in the 3rd Corps in Iraq during 2004, raised eyebrows after the Abu Ghraib scandal became public by choosing to eat meals with prison guards who, having been stigmatized in shame, usually found themselves eating alone. Chaplain Taylor befriended them and began trying to understand their experience. He asked them where the chaplain at Abu Ghraib had been during the abuses and if that chaplain's ministry had made any difference in their lives or to the culture of the prison.

Chaplain Taylor was disturbed by what he heard. It turned out that the chaplain for Abu Ghraib, a female lieutenant in the National Guard, was not originally part of the 800th Military Police Brigade but had been transferred to the prison after the Brigade had been there for some time. This made her an outsider to many of the guards. Moreover, this chaplain was of "Asian/ Pacific" descent and had a heavy accent. The guards who ate their meals with Chaplain Taylor complained that they often understood some of the prisoners better than they understood their own chaplain. As a result, chapel services at the prison rarely had more than a few dozen in attendance.

Yet the religious crisis at Abu Ghraib was due to a larger issue. As Chaplain Taylor pressed into the matter, he discovered that the chaplain had been told to stay out of the way, that her superiors instructed her to stay in her quarters and let soldiers with needs seek her out. She did as she was ordered, and the result was that the guards reported to Chaplain Taylor that they never saw the chaplain and that she simply wasn't a "player." In fact, not one of the guards reported ever engaging this chaplain in any way.

155

Taylor saw immediately what he had to do. When the 391st Military Police Battalion from Columbus, Ohio, took over at Abu Ghraib, he instructed the new chaplains to make themselves as present as possible in the lives and duties of the soldiers. This would do two things, he explained. First, soldiers would find the chaplains accessible and be more willing to engage them about their spiritual lives. Just as importantly, the chaplains would become what Taylor called a "moral influence by presence." He instructed the chaplains to be there at the change of shifts, when prisoners were moved, when interrogations took place, and as soldiers fulfilled the most mundane duties. Chaplain Gene Fowler, Taylor's superior officer, called this "ministry by presence," which means "taking the holy into the midst of the profane."

It worked. Both through the reforms that the military enacted to correct the scandals and through the proactive ministries of the new chaplains, Abu Ghraib has been transformed. Chaplain Taylor explained that there have been no further abuses and that, in fact, the prison has become a model success story. Attendance at chapel services reaches into the hundreds. Now, many of soldiers stationed at Abu Ghraib with the 391st carry medallions in their pockets that express their pride in the opportunity to live down the negative stigma of the prison. The slogan on the coin defines their newfound sense of mission. It says simply, "Restoring America's Honor."

Clearly, one of the benefits of a heartfelt warrior code is the restraint it provides to immoral behavior under the stress of war. There are other benefits, as we have seen: the ennobling of the profession at arms, the tempering of the informal warrior codes that arise from the informal faiths of the Millennials, and the greater zeal in the fight that a clear moral rationale produces. Each of these will be as necessary in the American wars to come as they have been in past conflicts.

Yet there is another benefit of a faith-based warrior code that is more needed today. A true warrior code assesses the enemy in moral, even religious, terms. It answers the religious claims of the opposition and infuses its warriors with the confidence that those claims are false. America will need this kind of warrior code more than ever in the years to come. This is because her primary enemy in the world is a religious network of terrorists that comes armed with a set of theological assumptions, with an assessment of the world in religious terms. To defeat this network, the United States will have to answer at both a theological and a military level.

This will mean taking the religious claims of the terrorists seriously, something that Americans have been largely unwilling to do. The terrorists, we are often told, are madmen. Because of their insanity, the mental dysfunction from which they suffer, nothing they say is of value. No one in their right mind would plan the murder of innocent thousands or commit suicide in the service of their faith. The result of such thinking is that the United States hunts down the terrorists but does

157

not address the religious claims that feed terrorism the world over. This is a tragic mistake.

The truth is that men like Osama bin Laden and the terrorists they lead are not at all insane. They are simply committed to an ideology fully at odds with Western culture and with the Christianity that gave birth to it. Osama bin Laden is, in fact, a highly intelligent man. His religious proclamations are far from the mindless rants they are often portrayed as. Instead, they are tightly reasoned expositions of the Quran that weigh Western culture and find it wanting. Through the lens of Muslim morality, Western culture is indeed a poisonous decadence that is due to receive the judgment of Allah. This bin Laden proclaims calmly and in a manner completely consistent with the teachings of the Quran.

Those who believed the September 11 terrorists to be madmen were challenged to think differently when the writings of the terrorists themselves came to light. In Muhammad Atta's apartment, the FBI found a diary that had been circulated among the terrorists prior to the attack. Out of respect for Allah, it says, clean your body, shave off excess hair, wear cologne, and tighten your shoes. Read the Quran and pray through the night in order to purify your soul from all unclean things. Try and detach yourself from this world because the time for play is over. Keep a steadfast mind because anything that happens to you could never be avoided, and what did not happen to you could never have happened to you. On the morning of the attack, pray the morning prayer and do not leave your apartment unless you have performed ablution. Pray as you enter the plane and recite verses from the Quran. Ask God to forgive your sins and to give you the victory. Clench your teeth as you prepare for the attack. Shout *Allahu Akbar.* Strike your enemy above the neck, as the Quran instructs. Moreover, if you slaughter, do not cause the discomfort of those you are killing, because this is one of the practices of the prophet, peace be upon him. Finally, you should feel complete tranquility, because the time between you and your marriage in heaven is very short.[2]

159

These words are not the rantings of an irrational terrorist. Instead, they are the calm reflections on impending death of a devoted, radical, fundamentalist Muslim. Muhammad Atta was not insane, nor were his followers. They were all Muslim warriors abiding by what may well be described as a Muslim warrior code as they visited what they believed to be Allah's judgment on the Great Satan. The truth is that they were moved to give us the horrors of September 11 by a very consistent body of thought, which in turn informed a carefully reasoned assessment of the United States.

This assessment was provided by the intellectual father of al-Qaeda, a man named Sayyid Qutb (pronounced 'Kuh-tahb'). Born in Egypt in 1906, Qutb had memorized the Quran by the age of ten and by his twenties was already writing novels and poems that captured the attention of the literary world. In the late 1940s he traveled to the United States and enrolled at the Colorado State College of Education to earn a master's degree. His experience in America at that time formed the basis for his assessment of Western culture, a perspective that has in turn framed the worldview of Osama bin Laden and al-Qaeda.

Qutb came to believe that America was a product of what he called a "hideous schizophrenia," by which he meant the separation of faith and life, church and state, religion and daily existence. As essayist Paul Berman has written for the *New York Times*: "The truly dangerous element in American life, in his [Qutb's] estimation, was not capitalism or foreign policy or racism or the unfortunate cult of women's independence. The truly dangerous element lay in America's separation of church and state—the modern political legacy of Christianity's ancient division between the sacred and the secular. This was not a political criticism. This was theological—though Qutb, or perhaps his translators, preferred the word 'ideological.'"[3]

Because in Qutb's view America had divorced the sacred from the secular, she had become a monster. Her men were weak, her women were immoral, her leaders were cowards, her thinking was muddled, and her entertainment was mindless vice. Her technological power and her media made her a font of wickedness in the world. Qutb came to believe the only answer for the world was a resurgence of Islam, the true faith that would again merge the sacred and the secular to bring human society under the rule of Allah. In a short book called *Milestones*, Qutb described his ideas in an impassioned but reasoned fashion. The book became the founding document of al-Qaeda and continues to frame the worldview of international terrorism to this day.[4]

161

The central point is that when Osama bin Laden and his ilk describe America as the Great Satan or speak of the United States as the source of evil in the world, it is not because they are unreasoning, irrational, or insane. It is because they are viewing the world through the lens of an ideology. This may distinguish the cool rage of al-Qaeda from the more volcanic anger toward America that lives in parts of the Muslim world because of U.S. support for Israel or the presence of U.S. troops in Saudi Arabia. Beyond the din of the angry Muslim crowd, though, the masterminds of international terrorism approach their task as the emissaries of God, as warrior/theologians bringing Allah's order to the earth.

A faith-based American warrior code would provide answers for those who must fight Muslim terrorists such as these. They are desperately needed. A young private who has been serving in the northern tribal regions of Afghanistan has found himself tormented by the image of the Great Satan he is told he represents. The words play over and over in his mind. "Our company got into some heavy fighting one day," he recalls, "and by the time we were done, some children were dead. I stared at their bodies while the women of the village—one of them was probably their mother—screamed at us. When I asked the interpreter what they were saying, she said they were telling us we were evil, that Satan was using us to destroy their lives. I went home and thought a lot about that. I'm having a hard time seeing how what they said is untrue."

An equally disturbing case is the story of a young Christian soldier serving in Iraq. Corporal Bob Daniels was converted to faith in Jesus Christ shortly before being called up with his National Guard unit in Tennessee. He has continued to feed his faith with the books and tapes of men like Jerry Falwell, Pat Robertson, and Rod Parsley. He likes what he hears from these men. It is clear, bold, and easy to understand. He especially appreciates what he hears about America. The country was founded as a Christian nation but has declined, and now immorality is rampant. There is abortion, nudity on television, widespread acceptance of homosexuality, and tragic ignorance of God's ways. America has to repent or God will judge her, and she will go the way of Sodom and Gomorrah.

But Bob Daniels is confused. He has recently read the Book of Habakkuk, and he knows that God sometimes uses a pagan people to deliver His judgment to a righteous nation. He wonders if God isn't using Muslim terrorists to judge America even though Islam is a false religion. Bob has thought about it a great deal. When he sits in the DFAC and listens to reports about Osama bin Laden's messages to the West on Fox television, he hears the same complaints about America that he hears from Falwell and Parsley. He hasn't been a Christian long, but it certainly sounds to him as though bin Laden himself may be speaking God's truth. If he is, could he be God's tool of judgment to bring America back to righteousness?

"I'm not completely sure yet," Daniels says, "but I'm beginning to wonder if the true Christians are on the wrong side of this thing. Maybe the terrorists are doing God's will. Maybe God wants to destroy the America that secular humanism built and restore her to be that

163

city on a hill she is supposed to be. I came over here all fired up thinking we were fighting against evil. Now I'm wondering if we are evil."

What Bob Daniels needs is what a faith-based warrior code would give him: an assessment of Islam that would frame his fight against terror. He does not need an extensive knowledge of Muslim theology. Yet he does need help understanding the difference between Islam and Islamic terrorism. He does need to see that Osama bin Laden's view of the West, which contains a morality somewhat similar to that of Christianity, is tied to a solution that would enslave most of the world. He needs to be able to hold a critical view of his nation's immorality without thinking that it lands him on the side of a terrorist network.

The reality is that ideas move too rapidly in our age not to arm the soldier in the field with at least the essential pillars of a worldview. A colonel at U.S. Central Command at MacDill Air Force Base rejects this idea. "If you think the average soldier is able to understand any of the complexities of Islam, you're fooling yourself. All you need to tell these guys is that they are fighting for freedom against tyranny, and they'll do the job. Anything else just gets in the way." Yet the very soldiers he would limit to a simplistic understanding of their fight sit in front of television sets in their off hours and watch debates of great complexity. For the first time in history, soldiers can shoot at their enemies in the afternoon and then return to camp to watch the English translation of an Al Jazeera broadcast and a debate on the floor of Congress the same evening. The new soldiers in the field have more information at their disposal than any who have fought under the American flag. What they need is a warrior code that gives them understanding of what they know and integrates that understanding into a worldview that helps them fight.

What is certain is that there has seldom been a time more ripe for a renewed emphasis on a faith-based warrior code. Though successful elections in Iraq bode well for the long-term prospects for democracy, it is clear that American troops will be needed to maintain stability for years to come. The same is true in Afghanistan where attacks on U.S. troops receive less press but continue to occur with frequency. Soldiers are becoming weary. There is a risk that they may lose their sense of mission. Respect for the cause of freedom and the welfare of civilians is becoming more difficult to maintain. A fresh emphasis on the noble calling of the warrior could save Americans the humiliation of yet another Abu Ghraib scandal.

165

Already the fabric of the American warrior profession is fraying. On February 2, 2005, Lieutenant General James Mattis told an audience in San Diego, California, exactly the opposite of what ought to inform a warrior ethos. Discussing the current wars in Afghanistan and Iraq, the general stated, "Actually it's quite fun to fight them, you know. It's a hoot. It's fun to shoot some people. I'll be right up there with you. I like brawling. You go into Afghanistan, you got guys who slap women around for five years because they didn't wear a veil. You know, guys like that ain't got no manhood left anyway. So it's sure a lot of fun to shoot them."[5]

Six days later, pictures appeared in the world press of female American soldiers mud wrestling and going topless at Camp Bucca in Iraq. Apparently a party celebrating the return of the 160th Military Police Battalion to the states got out of hand. Pictures of the October 30, 2004, event reached the press early in the new year.

Overlaying all of these revelations was a report late in January 2005 that interrogators at the Guantanamo Bay detention center tried to break Muslim detainees with sexual tactics. Former Army Sergeant Erik Saar, who was assigned to Guantanamo Bay, reported that Muslim detainees were interrogated by female civilian contractors wearing miniskirts, thongs, and other revealing clothing, an intentional violation of Muslim religious law that forbids close contact with women who are not their wives. Saar also reported that one of these female contractors smeared fake menstrual blood on a detainee and had the water turned off in the man's cell so that he could not wash. Muslim law forbids any male contact with a menstruating woman or with menstrual blood.[6]

These stories and others like them taint the image of the American military and seem to confirm the "Great Satan" suspicions of the nation's enemies. The young warriors in Afghanistan and Iraq today deserve better. They are, as we have seen, as patriotic, as religious, as intelligent, and as eager to do well in battle as any armed force the United States has sent into war. They deserve the honor of their country and the guarantee that whatever passes for their generation's My Lai massacres will not cause them to be unjustly despised. They are heroes and deserve the honor their nation accords her heroes.

Yet they are also deeply religious and in a thoroughly unstructured way. While the American military offers only the lightest ethos to guide them, they are fashioning their own warrior codes to serve the need all warriors have to understand their duties in the highest sense. This will prove to be one of the great challenges of the American military in the years to come: to integrate faith, discipline, heritage, ethics, and vision into a warrior code that fits the needs of this amazing new generation at war.

Wars may be fought with weapons, but

they are won by men. It is the spirit

of the men who follow and of the man

who leads that gains the victory.

—General George S. Patton
(1885–1945)

Epilogue

A band of Marines has just gathered in a small white trailer on an American base in Iraq. It is just moments before they go in search of insurgents in a nearby town. The mission will be dangerous. Each man knows this. They lost a buddy just days before, and this is one of the reasons that they have gathered now to offer themselves before their God.

Each would describe himself as Christian. One has been a Roman Catholic all his life. He carries a picture of the pope in his wallet, a crucifix around his neck, and has had the Jesuit crest tattooed upon his arm. There is another who has never set foot in a church but found the Jesus of his Christian friends in Iraq meeting him as he went into battle. When he saw *The Passion of the Christ* on a fellow soldier's notebook computer, he was hooked. He carries a Navy-issue copy of the New Testament in his vest and a folded scrap of paper with a verse from the Bible that he is trying to memorize. Two others are Baptists, one is barely Methodist, and another got halfway through an Episcopal seminary when the events of September 11, 2001, issued a different call.

They are standing in a circle now fully dressed for battle. They have brought all their gear with them and not just because they are about to go into the field. They want to present them before their God and ask His blessing on each item. During what follows, some will hold their rifle aloft as though to say, "Here, O Lord, receive this weapon into Your service."

There is no guide for what they are about to do. They have been given no liturgy, no handbook. Instead, they have evolved this ritual over the months they have fought together. They never intended to evolve anything. When they first met for a brief prayer before a mission, they did not know it would last. In fact, they were a bit hesitant about getting together even for a second time. One of them might be lost in battle, and it would be hard to gather without him. They got over this fear, though, and now they have pieced together a routine that is dear to them. It is, in truth, what brings them closer to God than anything they have ever known.

They begin with an ancient song. Because their bodies are thick with equipment and protective padding, they do not hug or join hands. Instead they merely touch the back of their gloved hands together as they stand in a circle and sing words that Christians have used in worship for centuries:

> Praise God from whom all blessings flow;
> Praise Him, all creatures here below;
> Praise Him above, ye heav'nly host;
> Praise Father, Son, and Holy Ghost.
> Amen.

Now they quote a scripture together. It is the same verse each time, and it comes from the story of King David. They have discussed the fact that when the people of God sinned in the Old Testament, their armies met with defeat. They would not have their sins

do likewise, so they quote together from David's ancient
song of repentance in Psalm 51:1–4, 10:

> Have mercy on me, O God,
> > according to your unfailing love;
> according to your great compassion
> > blot out my transgressions.
> Wash away all my iniquity
> > and cleanse me from my sin.
>
> For I know my transgressions,
> > and my sin is always before me.
> Against you, you only, have I sinned
> > and done what is evil in your sight,
> so that you are proved right when you
> > > speak
> > and justified when you judge....
>
> Create in me a pure heart, O God,
> > and renew a steadfast spirit within me.

When they finish reciting the words together in
husky, sincere voices, they pause in silence for each
man to confess his sins. It is usually at this point in
their informal liturgy that other Marines begin to step
quietly through their trailer door. They do not mean to
interfere, and they do not feel right about joining in. But
they do want to be as close to this font of faith as they

can get. So they stand in silence like an outer protective ring as the inner circle takes hold of God.

When enough moments for confession have passed, someone will begin to quote the words of Psalm 144:1–2, 5–6. It is often called the "Soldier's Psalm," and after one Marine starts it off, the others quickly join in:

> Praise be to the LORD my Rock,
>> who trains my hands for war,
>> my fingers for battle.
> He is my loving God and my fortress,
>> my stronghold and my deliverer,
> my shield, in whom I take refuge,
>> who subdues peoples under me....
> Part your heavens, O LORD, and come
>> down;
>> touch the mountains, so that they
>> smoke,
> Send forth lightning and scatter the
>> enemies;
>> shoot your arrows and rout them.

The Marines have only been circled together for a few moments, but there is a shuffling of feet as though someone feels that they are late. They are not. It is nerves. The words of Psalm 144 have turned thoughts to the fighting ahead, and this has made some antsy. It happens every time. But now comes the final song that draws their thoughts back to God. As the Marines in the circle begin to sing, they are aware that there is now a small band outside the trailer who draw near before each mission to sing this particular song. The words have been sung by Christians since knights left Europe to liberate the Holy Land. Everyone knows this. The Marine who almost finished seminary has told them the story, and now they all sing feeling at one with those knights of old and with soldiers at war through the centuries.

174

> Be Thou my Vision, O Lord of my heart;
> Naught be all else to me, save that Thou
>   art—
> Thou my best thought, by day or by night,
> Walking or sleeping, Thy presence my
>   light.
>
> High King of heaven, my victory won,
> May I reach heaven's joys, O bright
>   heav'n's Sun!
> Heart of my own heart, whatever befall,
> Still be my Vision, O Ruler of all.

Then, finally, a black Marine known for his sonorous voice leads a responsive declaration of Joshua 1:9.

While the men say the words in unison, some will kiss the little Shield of Strength from which the words come.

> I will be strong and courageous.
> I will not be terrified, or discouraged;
> For the Lord my God is with me
> Wherever I go.

When the black Marine says "Amen," all the others—those in the inner circle, those who entered the trailer late, and those who stand outside but eagerly join in—say "Amen" after him, and this is the sign to disband and move out.

175

There is not a man or a woman in this band over twenty-five. There is no chaplain present, nor has any church told them what to say. Yet these Millennials have fashioned together an expression both old and new that draws them near to God. They know that there is a spirituality to war, that warriors should trust in something beyond themselves to be of any use. So in the barrens of Iraq they build an altar of faith and ask their God to make them the warriors He has called them to be. So it is with the Vigil at Arms of a new generation. So it is with the faith of the new American soldier.

Notes

Chapter 1: The New Generation at War

1. Evan Wright, *Generation Kill* (New York: G. P. Putnam's Sons, 2004), 5.

2. Ibid., 6.

3. Victor Davis Hanson, "Anatomy of the Three-Week War," *National Review Online*, April 17, 2003, http://www .nationalreview.com/hanson/hanson/041703.asp (accessed February 21, 2005).

4. Harris Poll, *Harris Confidence Index*, January 22, 2003.

5. Institute of Politics, Harvard University, *A National Survey of College Undergraduates* (Cambridge, MA: Harvard University, 2002), 2.

6. Bell Irwin Wiley, *The Life of Johnny Reb: The Common Soldier of the Confederacy* (Indianapolis, IN: Wiley, 1943), 309.

7. Bell Irwin Wiley, *The Life of Billy Yank: The Common Soldier of the Union* (Indianapolis, IN: Wiley, 1952), 39–40.

8. Samuel A. Stouffer, et al., *The American Soldier: Combat and Its Aftermath*, vol. II (Princeton, NJ: Princeton University Press, 1949), 111.

9. *Why They Fight: Combat Motivation in the Iraq War*, Strategic Studies Institute, U.S. Army War College, July 2003, 17–18.

10. Ibid., 21.

11. John W. Brinsfield, *Encouraging Faith, Supporting Soldiers: The United States Army Chaplaincy, 1975–1995* (Washington DC: Department of the Army, Office of the Chief of Chaplains, 1997), part two, 155–156; Russell F. Weigley, *History of the United States Army* (New York: Macmillan Publishing Co., 1967), 519–520.

12. Chris Roberts, "Number of Single-Parent Families Increases 42%," *Columbia (SC) State*, May 23, 2001, A-1, A-12.

13. Neil Howe and William Strauss, *Millennials Rising: The Next Great Generation* (New York: Vintage Books, 2000), 14.

14. The Barna Group, www.barna.org.

15. Winston Churchill, *My Early Life* (New York: Scribner, 1977).

CHAPTER 2: SHIELDS OF STRENGTH

1. "Bush: 'This Nation Does Not Forget,'" CNN.com, Inside Politics, May 26, 2003, http://www.cnn.com/2003/ALLPOLITICS/05/26/bush.transcript/ (accessed February 22, 2005).

2. Arlington National Cemetery Website, Russell B. Rippetoe, Captain, United States Army, January 26, 2005, http://www.arlingtoncemetery.net/rbrippetoe.htm (accessed February 28, 2005).

CHAPTER 3: MEN OF CLOTH AND STEEL

1. The full story is told in Dan Kurzman's *No Greater Glory: The Four Immortal Chaplains and the Sinking of the Dorchester in WWII* (New York: Random House, 2004).

2. Ibid.

3. "Origins of the Chaplaincy," *A Brief History of the United States Chaplains Corp*, compiled by William J. Hourihan (Fort Jackson, SC: United States Army Chaplain Center and School), http://www.usachcs.army.mil/history/brief/chapter_1.htm (accessed February 24, 2005).

4. Ibid.

5. *Webster's Online Dictionary*, s.v. "John Peter Muhlenberg," http://www.websters-online-dictionary.org/definition/JOHN+PETER+MUHLENBERG (accessed February 25, 2005).

6. "Origins of the Chaplaincy," http://www.usachcs.army.mil/history/brief/chapter_1.htm (accessed February 24, 2005).

7. G. Cinton Prim, Jr., "Born Again in the Trenches: Revivals in the Army of Tennessee," *Tennessee Historical Quarterly* 43, no. 2 (984): 251.

8. Ibid.

9. Ibid., 253.

10. Ibid., 254.

11. Ibid., 259.

12. Ibid., 263.

13. Ibid., 269.

14. Ibid., 272.

15. "The United States Army Chaplaincy, 1865–1917," *A Brief History of the United States Chaplains Corp*, http://www .usachcs.army.mil/history/brief/chapter_4.htm (accessed February 24, 2005).

16. "World War I and Its Aftermath, 1917–1941," *A Brief History of the United States Chaplains Corp*, http://www .usachcs.army.mil/history/brief/chapter_5.htm (accessed February 24, 2005).

17. "World War II and Its Aftermath," *A Brief History of the United States Chaplains Corp*, http://www.usachcs .army.mil/history/brief/chapter_6.htm (accessed February 24, 2005).

18. H. A. DeWeerd, ed., *Selected Speeches and Statements of General of the Army George C. Marshall* (Washington DC: The Infantry Journal, 1945), 121–122.

19. "World War II and Its Aftermath," http://www .usachcs.army.mil/history/brief/chapter_6.htm (accessed February 24, 2005).

20. "The Cold War and the Chaplaincy," *A Brief History of the United States Chaplains Corp*, http://www.usachcs .army.mil/history/brief/chapter_7.htm (accessed February 24, 2005). Also, "Statistical Summary of America's Major Wars," United States Civil War Center, http://www.cwc .lsu.edu/cwc/other/stats/warcost.htm (accessed February 28, 2005).

21. "Bill Would Permit Military Academy Prayers," *Washington Times*, October 4, 2003.

CHAPTER 4: ANVIL OF THE WARRIOR CODE

1. *The Micah Mandate*, vol. 11, issue 2, Elijah Ministries, February 1996, http://www.mttu.com/elijahmin/Archives/ Volume%2011%20Issue%202%20-%20February%201996 .htm (accessed February 25, 2005).

181

2. Robert Patterson, *Dereliction of Duty* (Washington DC: Regnery Publishing, 2003).

3. Ibid., 145–146.

4. *A Few Good Men*, screenplay by Aaron Sorkin, directed by Rob Reiner, 1992.

5. Ibid.

6. "The Leader and Leadership: What the Leader Must Be, Know, and Do," FM 22-100, http://atiam.train.army .mil/portal/atia/adlsc/view/public/296756-1/fm/22-100/ch2 .htm (accessed February 24, 2005).

7. "The Way Ahead: Our Army at War, Relevant and Ready," U.S. Army, http://www.army.mil/thewayahead/creed.html (accessed February 24, 2005).

8. "Washington's Farewell Address 1796," The Avalon Project at Yale Law School, http://www.yale.edu/lawweb/avalon/washing.htm (accessed February 24, 2005).

9. Augustine of Hippo, *The City of God* (New York: Doubleday, 1958), 447.

10. Ibid.

11. President's Remarks at National Day of Prayer and Remembrance," September 14, 2001, http://www.whitehouse.gov/news/releases/2001/09/20010914-2.html (accessed February 24, 2005).

12. "Be Ye Men of Valour," *National Geographic*, August 1965, 159.

CHAPTER 5: BREAKING CODE

1. James R. Schlesinger, et al., *Final Report of the Independent Panel to Review DOD Detention Operations* (Arlington, VA: 2004), 75. Available at http://wid.ap.org/documents/iraq/040824finalreport.pdf#search='Schlesinger%20report' (accessed February 25, 2005).

2. "Notes Found After the Hijackings," *New York Times*, September 29, 2001, B-3.

3. Paul Berman, "The Philosopher of Islamic Terror," *New York Times*, March 23, 2003, www.nytimes.com/2003/03/23/magazine/23GURU.html (accessed February 25, 2005).

4. Sayyid Qutb, *Milestones* (Beirut: The Holy Quran Publishing House, 1980). Available online at Young Muslims, http://www.youngmuslims.ca/online_library/books/milestones/ (accessed February 25, 2005).

5. John J. Lumpkin, "Marine General Says It's 'Fun' to Shoot Some in Combat," Associated Press, February 4, 2005.

6. Carol D. Leonnig and Dana Priest, "Detainees Accuse Female Interrogators," *Washington Post*, February 10, 2005, http://www.washingtonpost.com/ac2/wp-dyn/A12431-2005Feb9?language=printer (accessed February 25, 2005).

Bibliography

"Be Ye Men of Valour." *National Geographic*, August 1965.

"Bill Would Permit Military Academy Prayers." *Washington Times*, October 4, 2003.

"Notes Found After the Hijackings." *New York Times*, September 29, 2001, sec. B.

"The Leader and Leadership: What the Leader Must Be, Know, and Do." FM 22-100, http://atiam.train.army.mil/portal/atia/adlsc/view/public/296756-1/fm/22-100/ch2.htm (accessed February 24, 2005).

"The Way Ahead: Our Army at War, Relevant and Ready." U.S. Army, http://www.army.mil/thewayahead/creed.html (accessed February 24, 2005).

"Washington's Farewell Address 1796." The Avalon Project at Yale Law School, http://www.yale.edu/lawweb/avalon/washing.htm (accessed February 24, 2005).

Augustine of Hippo, *The City of God*. New York: Doubleday, 1958.

Berman, Paul. "The Philosopher of Islamic Terror." *New York Times*, March 23, 2003, sec. 6, www.nytimes

.com/2003/03/23/magazine/23GURU.html (accessed February 25, 2005).

Brinsfield, John W. *Encouraging Faith, Supporting Soldiers: The United States Army Chaplaincy, 1975–1995*, part two. Washington DC: Department of the Army, Office of the Chief of Chaplains, 1997).

Churchill, Winston. *My Early Life*. New York: Scribner, 1977.

CNN.com. "Bush: 'This Nation Does Not Forget.'" Inside Politics, May 26, 2003, http://www.cnn.com/2003/ALLPOLITICS/05/26/bush.transcript/ (accessed February 22, 2005).

DeWeerd, H. A., ed. *Selected Speeches and Statements of General of the Army George C. Marshall*. Washington DC: The Infantry Journal, 1945.

Elijah Ministries. *The Micah Mandate*. Vol. 11, issue 2, February 1996, http://www.mttu.com/elijahmin/Archives/Volume%2011%20Issue%202%20-%20February%201996.htm (accessed February 25, 2005).

Hanson, Victor Davis. "Anatomy of the Three-Week War." *National Review Online*, April 17, 2003, http://www.nationalreview.com/hanson/hanson/041703.asp (accessed February 21, 2005).

Harris Poll. *Harris Confidence Index*, January 22, 2003.

Hourihan, William J., compiler. "Origins of the Chaplaincy." *A Brief History of the United States Chaplains Corp*. Fort

Jackson, SC: United States Army Chaplain Center and School, http://www.usachcs.army.mil/history/brief/chapter_1.htm (accessed February 24, 2005).

_____. "The Cold War and the Chaplaincy." *A Brief History of the United States Chaplains Corp*. Fort Jackson, SC: United States Army Chaplain Center and School, http://www.usachcs.army.mil/history/brief/chapter_7.htm (accessed February 24, 2005).

_____. "The United States Army Chaplaincy, 1865–1917." *A Brief History of the United States Chaplains Corp*. Fort Jackson, SC: United States Army Chaplain Center and School, http://www.usachcs.army.mil/history/brief/chapter_4.htm (accessed February 24, 2005).

_____. "World War I and Its Aftermath, 1917–1941." *A Brief History of the United States Chaplains Corp*. Fort Jackson, SC: United States Army Chaplain Center and School, http://www.usachcs.army.mil/history/brief/chapter_5.htm (accessed February 24, 2005).

_____. "World War II and Its Aftermath." *A Brief History of the United States Chaplains Corp*. Fort Jackson, SC: United States Army Chaplain Center and School, http://www.usachcs.army.mil/history/brief/chapter_6.htm (accessed February 24, 2005).

Howe, Neil, and William Strauss. *Millennials Rising: The Next Great Generation*. New York: Vintage Books, 2000.

Institute of Politics. *A National Survey of College Undergraduates*. Cambridge, MA: Harvard University, 2002.

Kurzman, Dan. *No Greater Glory: The Four Immortal Chaplains and the Sinking of the Dorchester in WWII.* New York: Random House, 2004.

Leonnig, Carol D., and Dana Priest, "Detainees Accuse Female Interrogators," *Washington Post*, February 10, 2005, http://www.washingtonpost.com/ac2/wp-dyn/A12431-2005Feb9?language=printer (accessed February 25, 2005).

Lumpkin, John. "Marine General Says It's 'Fun' to Shoot Some in Combat." Associated Press, February 4, 2005.

Patterson, Robert. *Dereliction of Duty.* Washington DC: Regnery Publishing, 2003.

Prim, G. Clinton Jr. "Born Again in the Trenches: Revivals in the Army." *Tennessee Historical Quarterly* 43, no. 3 (1984).

Qutb, Sayyid. *Milestones.* Beirut, Lebanon: The Holy Quran Publishing House, 1980. Available online at Young Muslims, http://www.youngmuslims.ca/online_library/books/milestones/ (accessed February 25, 2005).

Roberts, Chris. "Number of Single-Parent Families Increases 42%." *Columbia (SC) State.* May 23, 2001, sec. A.

Schlesinger, James R., et al., *Final Report of the Independent Panel to Review DOD Detention Operations.* Arlington, VA: 2004, http://wid.ap.org/documents/iraq/040824finalreport.pdf#search='Schlesinger%20report' (accessed February 25, 2005).

Stouffer, Samuel A., et al. *The American Soldier: Combat and Its Aftermath*, vol. II. Princeton, NJ: Princeton University Press, 1949.

Strategic Studies Institute. *Why They Fight: Combat Motivation in the Iraq War*. U.S. Army War College, July 2003.

Webster's Online Dictionary, s.v. "John Peter Muhlenberg," http://www.websters-online-dictionary.org/definition/ JOHN+PETER+MUHLENBERG (accessed February 25, 2005).

Weigley, Russell F. *History of the United States Army*. New York: Macmillan Publishing Co., 1967.

White House, "President's Remarks at National Day of Prayer and Remembrance," September 14, 2001, http:// www.whitehouse.gov/news/releases/2001/09/20010914 -2.html (accessed February 24, 2005).

Wiley, Bell Irwin. *The Life of Billy Yank: The Common Soldier of the Union*. Indianapolis, IN: Wiley, 1952.

_____. *The Life of Johnny Reb: The Common Soldier of the Confederacy*. Indianapolis, IN: Wiley, 1943.

Wright, Evan. *Generation Kill*. New York: G. P. Putnam's Sons, 2004.

ACKNOWLEDGMENTS

It was Theodore Roosevelt who said, "Far better it is to dare mighty things, to win glorious triumphs, even though checkered with failure, than to take rank with those poor spirits who neither enjoy much or suffer much because they live in the grey twilight that knows not victory nor defeat." I think of our warriors in Afghanistan and Iraq when I hear this quote now. They have dared mighty things, and they will know their failures and defeats, but they will, I believe, force history to remember the greatness of their generation at war. They are my heroes, and I honor them first of all in these acknowledgments, just as I hope I have honored them with this book.

Among them were those who graciously tended me in Iraq. LTC Hunt Kerrigan, Chaplain (COL) Gene Fowler, and Chaplain (LTC) Daniel Taylor each made me welcome and took time to help me understand their world. SGT Mark Shannon made sure I saw the grit of war and introduced me to those amazing kids in the 1544th Transportation Company. How much poorer my life and this book would have been without them. Also making my time in Iraq possible were Bruce Zielsdorf, Dave Ballengee, CPT David Tippett, CPT Joseph Edstrom, Chaplain John D. Read, and MAJ Kris Meyle. You are all remembered with gratitude.

It was LTC James Carter who invited me to explore the warrior code at the United States Military Academy. He introduced me to such valiant souls as BG Scapparotti, Dr. Don Snider, LTC Jon Smidt, COL Scott McChrystal, MAJ Carlos Huerta, MAJ Darrell Thomsen, Cadet First Captain Ryan Boeka, Dr. John

Brinsfield, and the beautiful Tiger family. Each made a deposit onto these pages and into my soul. Thank you.

BG (RET) Howard Prince, formerly of West Point and currently of the LBJ School of Public Affairs at the University of Texas, took time to help me understand Abu Ghraib and the parallels with the Stanford Prison Experiment in 1971. He was patient with my ignorance and kind as great teachers always are. Chaplain (LTC) Dave West was the Deputy Command Chaplain at U.S. Central Command in Florida when he graciously took time to help me understand the world of the combat chaplain. Both of these men bring honor to their profession.

It was the generosity of my publishers, Tarcher Penguin and Charisma House, that allowed me to go to Iraq to dig out the stories in this book. They have been wise and caring allies, much as they were when we worked together on *The Faith of George W. Bush.* The editorial skills of Barbara Dycus at Charisma House and Mitch Horowitz at Tarcher Penguin have made this book far more than I could have made it on my own. I cannot fail to mention Ken Siman, also of Tarcher Penguin, who is a delight to know and to work with.

My own team at The Mansfield Group have again been at my side and have again brought their astonishing skills into harness for one of my projects. Though he was going through a cruel season of his own, George

Grant has given me wise counsel and the benefits of his brilliant scholarship once again. He is both a dear friend and a beloved comrade in arms whose recent struggles remind me of the words of Washington Irving: "There is nothing so baleful to a small man as the shade of a great one."

Eric Holmberg has a passion for truth that exceeds my own and, though he was engaged with important projects of his own, gave himself to the research for this book with insight and skill. His wife, Ronda, has also shaped this book both with her passion and her mastery of the art of the interview. Though their friendship is dearer to me than their scholarly gifts, I am thankful that they have graced me with both once again.

Beverly Darnall, executive director of Chartwell Literary Group, served as the public affairs officer for this book. She tirelessly pursued the permission we needed to land me in Iraq, and her skills in navigating the mysterious ways of the Pentagon paid off in many of the treasures that are in these pages. Her brilliance as a project manager and her wisdom as an editor have also helped make this book much of what it is, and I am, once more, in her debt.

LTC Ken Lewis has been my military affairs advisor, and, though every mistake is certainly mine, he has helped me sound less like an idiot than I might have. His education at West Point and his experience as an Army Ranger—not to mention his time at U.S. Central Command and in Qatar during the writing of this book—have been of inestimable value to me. He is always patient and always informed, and it only increases my love for him that besides being my friend, he is also my brother-in-law.

Sam Chappell runs my world with vision, and though I abuse him regularly, he has made a huge difference in my life. It was his idea for The Mansfield Group to build an alliance with the Ambassador Speaker's Bureau, and this partnership—as well as the friendships with Wes Yoder, Dana Ashley, and the gang—allowed me to fulfill a good number of my dreams. Susan Levine has served us all with her amazing skills, and this despite the loss of Carl, the love of her life. Thank you, my dear.

I cannot end without again expressing deep love for my spiritual family. Rice Broocks, Jim Laffoon, Brett Fuller, Ron Lewis, and, always, Coach Rohr have changed me, and I can only hope that my life will do justice to their wise and rugged care for my soul. A man could have no better band of brothers.

About the Author

Stephen Mansfield first acquired his sense of honor for the American soldier from his family history. His father fought in Vietnam, his grandfather was paralyzed in the assault on Berlin during World War II, and members of his family have been fighting for their country since the American Revolution.

His love of things military has moved him to earn a master's degree in history and public policy and a doctorate in history and literature. His writing has also centered around themes of war and leadership. His first book, *Never Give In: The Extraordinary Character of Winston Churchill*, was a Gold Medallion Book Award finalist in 1995. His ground-breaking *The Faith of George W. Bush* was not only a *New York Times* bestseller in 2003 but also has been credited with profoundly shaping public discourse on faith and American culture.

Mansfield lectures widely throughout the United States and abroad, leads a successful research and publishing firm called The Mansfield Group, and, in his spare time, feeds a wicked addiction to racquetball and travel.

His website is: www.mansfieldgroup.com